Jira Software Essentials

Second Edition

Plan, track, and release great applications with Jira Software

Patrick Li

BIRMINGHAM - MUMBAI

Jira Software Essentials
Second Edition

Commissioning Editor: Richa Tripathi
Acquisition Editor: Nitin Dasan
Content Development Editor: Nikhil Borkar
Technical Editor: Jijo Maliyekal
Copy Editor: Safis Editing
Project Coordinator: Ulhas Kambali
Proofreader: Safis Editing
Indexer: Francy Puthiry
Graphics: Tania Dutta
Production Coordinator: Shantanu Zagade

First published: June 2015
Second edition: January 2018

Production reference: 1250118

Published by Packt Publishing Ltd.
Livery Place
35 Livery Street
Birmingham
B3 2PB, UK.

ISBN 978-1-78883-351-6

www.packtpub.com

`mapt.io`

Mapt is an online digital library that gives you full access to over 5,000 books and videos, as well as industry leading tools to help you plan your personal development and advance your career. For more information, please visit our website.

Why subscribe?

- Spend less time learning and more time coding with practical eBooks and Videos from over 4,000 industry professionals

- Improve your learning with Skill Plans built especially for you

- Get a free eBook or video every month

- Mapt is fully searchable

- Copy and paste, print, and bookmark content

PacktPub.com

Did you know that Packt offers eBook versions of every book published, with PDF and ePub files available? You can upgrade to the eBook version at `www.PacktPub.com` and as a print book customer, you are entitled to a discount on the eBook copy. Get in touch with us at `service@packtpub.com` for more details.

At `www.PacktPub.com`, you can also read a collection of free technical articles, sign up for a range of free newsletters, and receive exclusive discounts and offers on Packt books and eBooks.

Contributors

About the author

Patrick Li is the cofounder of AppFusions and now works as a senior engineer there. He has worked in the Atlassian ecosystem for over ten years, developing products and solutions, and providing expert consulting services across verticals such as healthcare, software engineering, financial services, and government agencies. He has authored numerous books and video courses covering Atlassian Jira, from versions 4 to 7, including Jira Agile (now Jira Software) and Jira Service Desk.

I would like to thank my wife Katherine, who has supported and encouraged me along the way, starting from the very first book. I would also like to thank all the reviewers for their valuable feedbacks, and also the publishers/coordinators, for their help to make this happen.

About the reviewer

Miroslav Kralik is a product owner and DevOps evangelist at MSD IT Global Innovation Center (known as Merck in the US and Canada). He focuses on DevOps and integration of different tools in the entire development chain, where Jira belongs as an issue and bug tracking system. One of his responsibilities is to promote the DevOps culture and tools in the company in the form of writing good practices and conducting training sessions, evangelism, and workshops (onsite/remote) in US, Asia, and Europe.

Packt is searching for authors like you

If you're interested in becoming an author for Packt, please visit `authors.packtpub.com` and apply today. We have worked with thousands of developers and tech professionals, just like you, to help them share their insight with the global tech community. You can make a general application, apply for a specific hot topic that we are recruiting an author for, or submit your own idea.

Table of Contents

Preface

Agile software development is a new and revolutionary way of developing software. Many organizations have adopted agile over the traditional waterfall model, as it lets development teams to produce software of better quality, higher customer satisfaction, and improved efficiency. Jira Software brings the power of agile to Atlassian Jira, the most popular enterprise issue tracking and project management system.

With Jira Software, you will be able to enjoy all the features you love with Jira, such as custom fields and flexible workflows, and also use agile to manage and run your projects.

Who this book is for

If you want to get started with using agile with Jira Software, then this is the perfect book for you. Perhaps, you have used agile to run your projects before or are just looking to try agile out—Jira Software is the perfect tool to get started.

You will need to be familiar with the basics of Jira, both from an end user's perspective and an administrator's perspective. Experience with workflows, custom fields, and other administrative functions of Jira will be useful. Prior experience with agile is not required but is useful.

What this book covers

This book is organized into seven chapters, starting with an overview of Jira Software and how to install the software. We then move on to introducing the two main agile methodologies, Scrum and Kanban, and how to use Jira Software with them. In the last two chapters, we go beyond the basics and look at ways to further customize Jira Software to extract more value out of it.

With each chapter, you will learn important concepts, including the agile methodologies themselves and how Jira Software lets you take advantage of them.

Chapter 1, *Jira Software Basics*, serves as the starting point of the book and aims to guide you through installing the Jira Software and getting it up and running. This chapter is also a gentle introduction, covering the basic concepts and terminologies used in Jira Software, and will lay the foundation for subsequent chapters.

Chapter 2, *Jira Software for Scrum*, covers using Jira Software for the Scrum methodology, starting with a high-level overview of Scrum, and then describes how Jira Software can be used to run projects with Scrum.

Chapter 3, *Jira Software for Kanban*, covers using Jira Software for the Kanban methodology. This chapter starts with an introduction to Kanban and how to use Jira Software to run Kanban-based projects.

Chapter 4, *Using Jira Software Your Way*, extends the previous chapter by introducing some of the additional customizations available for running Scrum projects with Jira Software. This chapter covers some of the key customization options, including board column layout and swimlanes.

Chapter 5, *Customizing Jira Software*, covers the non-agile customizations that you can have for Jira Software. These cover the features that Jira Software provides for you to have your own custom fields, screen layouts, and workflows.

Chapter 6, *Jira Software – Advanced*, covers some advanced uses of Jira Software, including additional customization options, and how to integrate Jira Software with Atlassian Confluence and third-party add-ons. By integrating Jira Software with these additional tools, teams can be more effective at creating content and reporting project progress, and can go beyond the out-of-box features.

Chapter 7, *Jira Software – Release and Deploy*, covers using Jira Software with Atlassian Bamboo to automate, build, release, and deploy processes.

To get the most out of this book

Since Jira Agile is an add-on extension to Atlassian Jira, you will need a running installation of Jira. You can download and install the latest version of Jira at `http://www.atlassian.com/software/jira/download`.

Jira and the additional add-on Agile Cards for Jira, used in Chapter 5, *Customizing Jira Software*, can be downloaded and installed them from inside the Jira application. However, if your Jira installation does not have access to the internet, you can download Jira Agile from `https://marketplace.atlassian.com/plugins/com.pyxis.greenhopper.jira` and Agile Cards for Jira from `https://marketplace.atlassian.com/plugins/com.spartez.scrumprint.scrumplugin`.

Conventions used

There are a number of text conventions used throughout this book.

`CodeInText`: Indicates code words in text, database table names, folder names, filenames, file extensions, pathnames, dummy URLs, user input, and Twitter handles. Here is an example: "the JQL query of `fixVersioninunreleasedVersions()ORfixVersionisEMPTY`."

Bold: Indicates a new term, an important word, or words that you see onscreen. For example, words in menus or dialog boxes appear in the text like this. Here is an example: "**Sample Kanban Board** is using the **Filter for Sample Kanban Project** saved filter."

Warnings or important notes appear like this.

Tips and tricks appear like this.

Get in touch

Feedback from our readers is always welcome.

General feedback: Email `feedback@packtpub.com` and mention the book title in the subject of your message. If you have questions about any aspect of this book, please email us at `questions@packtpub.com`.

Errata: Although we have taken every care to ensure the accuracy of our content, mistakes do happen. If you have found a mistake in this book, we would be grateful if you would report this to us. Please visit `www.packtpub.com/submit-errata`, selecting your book, clicking on the Errata Submission Form link, and entering the details.

Piracy: If you come across any illegal copies of our works in any form on the Internet, we would be grateful if you would provide us with the location address or website name. Please contact us at `copyright@packtpub.com` with a link to the material.

If you are interested in becoming an author: If there is a topic that you have expertise in and you are interested in either writing or contributing to a book, please visit `authors.packtpub.com`.

Reviews

Please leave a review. Once you have read and used this book, why not leave a review on the site that you purchased it from? Potential readers can then see and use your unbiased opinion to make purchase decisions, we at Packt can understand what you think about our products, and our authors can see your feedback on their book. Thank you!

For more information about Packt, please visit `packtpub.com`.

1
Jira Software Basics

Agile software development has been gaining momentum over the years as more and more people start to see problems with the traditional model, and the benefits that agile methodologies bring. In agile methods, development happens in iterative cycles and improvements are made with each iteration. Feedback is gathered as early as possible, improving customer engagement and team collaboration. All these actions make development teams better at anticipating and managing changes.

Atlassian, the maker of the popular issue-tracking software Jira, recognizes the values that agile methods can bring, and has come out with a solution that is specially designed for managing projects using agile with Jira, called Jira Software. In this chapter, we will introduce the basics of Jira Software.

By the end of the chapter, you will have learned about:

- Jira Software and what it offers
- How to install and configure a new instance of Jira Software
- The key concepts and terminologies of Jira Software
- How to create new agile projects with project templates

Introducing Jira Software

Jira Software, one of the three products in the Jira product family, along with Jira Core and Jira Service Desk, is a solution that is primarily focused on managing software development projects using agile methodologies, hence the name Jira Software. It takes some of the features of classic Jira (Jira Core), such as customizable fields and flexible workflows, and combines them with support for agile methods, giving you the complete experience of running a project the agile way.

Out of the box, Jira Software supports the following agile methodologies:

- **Scrum**: This is an agile methodology where the development team works iteratively to complete the project. Each iteration or sprint has a defined timeframe and scope. Scrum is most suitable for software development projects. You can find out more about Scrum at `http://en.wikipedia.org/wiki/Scrum_(software_development)`.
- **Kanban**: This is an agile methodology that focuses on just-in-time delivery by visualizing the workflow and tasks in progress. Kanban is most suitable for operation teams. You can find out more about Kanban at `http://en.wikipedia.org/wiki/Kanban`.

Of course, since Jira Software is bundled with Jira Core, you also have the option to use Jira without agile methods, such as using it as a simple task tracker, and manage non-software-development-related projects. While we will be focusing mostly on using Jira Software for agile purposes, many of the concepts and topics, especially from Chapter 5, *Customizing Jira Software*, onwards, are also applicable to non-agile-based projects. Given that we are specifically covering Jira Software in this book, we will be using the terms **Jira** and **Jira Software** interchangeably, unless explicitly stated otherwise.

Installing Jira Software

Often, the best way to get familiar with something is to be hands-on, so we will be installing an instance of Jira Software and using that as the basis for all our subsequent chapters and exercises.

Installing Jira Software is a straightforward process. All you need are:

- A server or virtual machine running either Windows or Linux
- A database: Oracle, MySQL, Microsoft SQL Server, or PostgreSQL
- Oracle JDK 1.8 or newer
- The Jira Software installation package

You can find the full list of supported platforms and systems at `https://confluence.atlassian.com/adminjiraserver075/supported-platforms-9353908 28.html`.

Obtaining and installing Jira Software

For this section, we will be using the TAR.GZ or ZIP Archive installation package, as it works with any operating system. You can download the latest Jira Software from `https://www.atlassian.com/software/jira/download`. By default, the download page will autoselect an installation package based on the operating system used by your computer. You can click on the **All Server versions** link to see all options.

Once you have downloaded the file, go through the following steps to install Jira Software:

1. Unzip the installation package (for example, `atlassian-jira-software-7.5.0.tar.gz`) to the location in which you want to install Jira Software. For example, in Linux, you might want to install it under the `/opt` directory. We will be referring to this directory as `JIRA_INSTALL` for the remainder of the book.

2. Make sure the startup script file in the `bin` directory is executable. For Linux, it will be `start-jira.sh`; for Windows, it will be `start-jira.bat`.

 Make sure you create a user to run Jira Software with. You should not run the application under default admin accounts, such as root.

3. Create a separate directory for Jira to store its local files, such as configurations, and logs. Make sure you keep this directory separate and outside the `JIRA_INSTALL` directory. Jira refers to this directory as `jira.home`, so we will be referring to this directory as `JIRA_HOME` for the remainder of the book.

4. Open the file `jira-application.properties` in a text editor. You can find the file under the `JIRA_INSTALL/atlassian-jira/WEB-INF/classes` directory.

5. Enter the full path of the `JIRA_HOME` directory. So the content of the file will look something like:
   `jira.home = /opt/jira_home`

6. Save the file and execute the appropriate startup script in the `bin` directory from a console. You should see an output in your console similar to the following screenshot:

```
●  ●  ●                              bin — -bash — 153×43
                    /opt/atlassian-jira-software-7.5.0-standalone/bin — -bash                          +
Last login: Sat Oct 21 17:33:49 on ttys001
MacBook-Pro-6:~ lulumomo$ cd /opt/atlassian-jira-software-7.5.0-standalone/bin/
MacBook-Pro-6:bin lulumomo$ ./start
start-jira.sh  startup.sh
MacBook-Pro-6:bin lulumomo$ ./start-jira.sh

To run JIRA in the foreground, start the server with start-jira.sh -fg
executing as current user
              ......
       ..... .NMMMMD.  ...
        .8MMM.  $MMN,..~MMMO.
        .?MMM.        .MMM?.

    OMMMMZ.              .,NMMMN~
   .IMMMMMM. .NMMMN. .MMMMMN,
    ,MMMMMMs..3MD..ZMMMMMM.
     =NMMMMMM,. .,MMMMMMD.
      .MMMMMMMM8MMMMMMMM,
        .ONMMMMMMMMMMMZ.
          ,NMMMMMMMM8.
          .:,.$MMMMMMM
        .IMMMM..NMMMMMD.
        .8MMMMM:  :NMMMMN.
        .MMMMMM.   .MMMMM~.
        .MMMMMN    .MMMMM?.


      Atlassian JIRA
      Version : 7.5.0


If you encounter issues starting or stopping JIRA, please see the Troubleshooting guide at http://confluence.atlassian.com/display/JIRA/Installation+Trou
bleshooting+Guide


Server startup logs are located in /opt/atlassian-jira-software-7.5.0-standalone/logs/catalina.out
Using CATALINA_BASE:   /opt/atlassian-jira-software-7.5.0-standalone
Using CATALINA_HOME:   /opt/atlassian-jira-software-7.5.0-standalone
Using CATALINA_TMPDIR: /opt/atlassian-jira-software-7.5.0-standalone/temp
Using JRE_HOME:        /Library/Java/JavaVirtualMachines/jdk1.8.0_51.jdk/Contents/Home
Using CLASSPATH:       /opt/atlassian-jira-software-7.5.0-standalone/bin/bootstrap.jar:/opt/atlassian-jira-software-7.5.0-standalone/bin/tomcat-juli.jar
Using CATALINA_PID:    /opt/atlassian-jira-software-7.5.0-standalone/work/catalina.pid
Tomcat started.
MacBook-Pro-6:bin lulumomo$ ▊
```

Setting up Jira Software

Now that we have installed Jira, we need to set it up by configuring its locale, language, and other aspects of the system. Jira comes with a setup wizard that will help guide us through the process.

We can access the wizard by opening up a browser and going to `http://localhost:8080`. This is if you are accessing Jira from the same machine that it is installed on. If you are using a different computer, change `localhost` to the actual host name. If Jira started up successfully, you should see the first step of the Jira setup wizard, as shown in the following screenshot. The **Set it up for me** option is a quick way for Jira to configure itself automatically, and this is a great way to have a trial environment up and running quickly. We will be using the **I'll set it up myself** option in this exercise to explore all the options available:

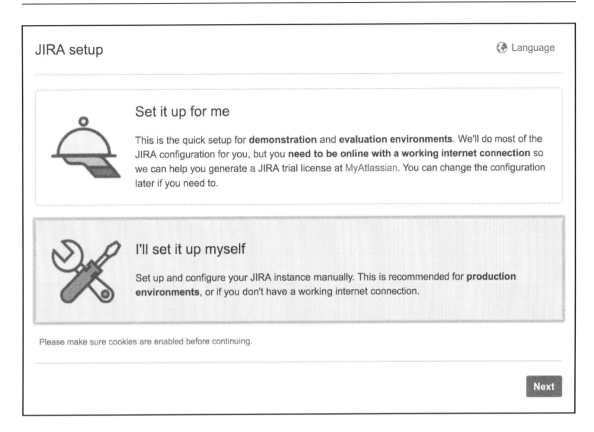

The second step is where we tell Jira the type of database we will be using and how to connect to it. The **Built In** option will create an in-memory database, which is useful for quick trials, but if you want to use Jira in production, you need to select the **My Own Database** option.

Select the database type you want to use. Note that for some databases, such as MySQL, you will be required to download the driver and install the driver before you can proceed further. Jira will let you know if a driver is needed.

Once you have selected the database type, enter the connectivity details. Each database type is different, so you will need to consult with your DBA or database manual if you are unsure. Use the **Test Connection** button to check whether the settings are correct and Jira is able to connect to the database.

Sometimes network configurations or firewall rules may prevent Jira from connecting to the database:

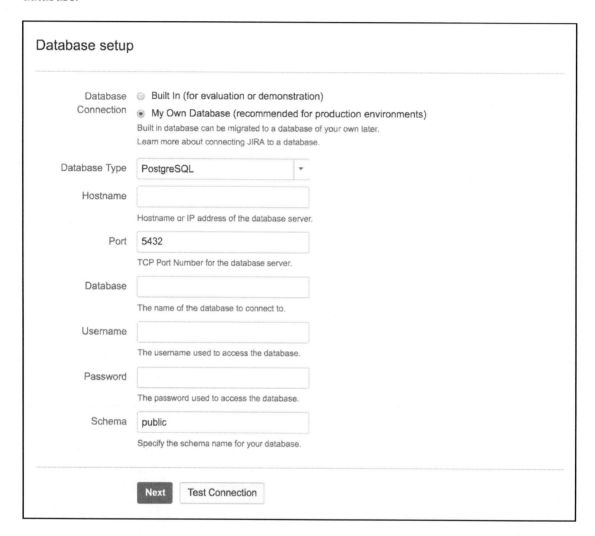

The third step is for you to enter some basic information about your Jira installation. All these settings can be changed later, so do not worry if you are not sure. The one setting to take note of is **Base URL**. It needs to be the fully qualified URL to your Jira instance. If this is set incorrectly, it may lead to issues later, such as links in email notifications not working:

Set up application properties

Existing data? You can import your data from another installed or hosted JIRA server instead of completing this setup process.

Application Title	Your Company JIRA
	The name of this installation.
Mode	⦿ Private
	Only administrators can create new users.
	◯ Public
	Anyone can sign up to create issues.
Base URL	http://localhost:8080
	The base URL for this installation of JIRA. All links created will be prefixed by this URL.

Next

The fourth step is where you enter your license key for Jira Software. If you have a key, simply cut and paste it into the text box. If you do not have one, you can generate a 30-day trial license by clicking the **generate a JIRA trial license** link on the page.

This will require you to have an account with the My Atlassian portal. If you do not already have an account, you can register one for free and then generate a trial license:

Specify your license key

You need a license key to set up JIRA. Enter your license key or generate a new license key below. You need an account at MyAtlassian to generate a license key.

Please enter your license key

> Server ID **B4EO-ET3W-O83E-8002**

Your License Key

> or generate a JIRA trial license at MyAtlassian

`Next`

For the fifth step, you will be asked to create the administrator account. This will be the super administrator account that you will need during emergencies, especially if you integrate Jira with an external user management system, such as LDAP, and there is a problem with the connectivity between you and your chosen management system.

 Store the credential of this account in a safe place and do not lose it.

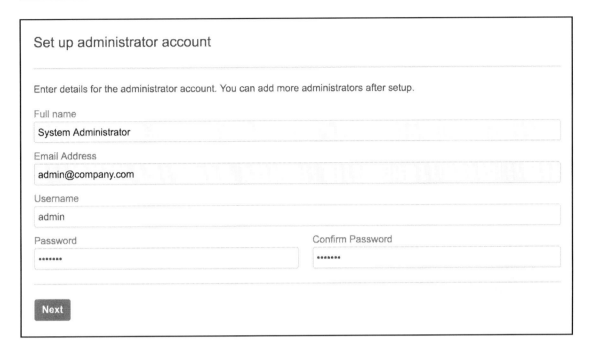

For the sixth and last step, you have the opportunity to set up how Jira will be sending out emails for notifications. Unlike the previous steps, this is optional, so if you do not have a mail server ready, you can skip this step and set it up later:

And that is it! Congratulations, your Jira is installed, configured, and ready to be used. Click on the **Take me to JIRA** button at the bottom-right corner to exit the wizard:

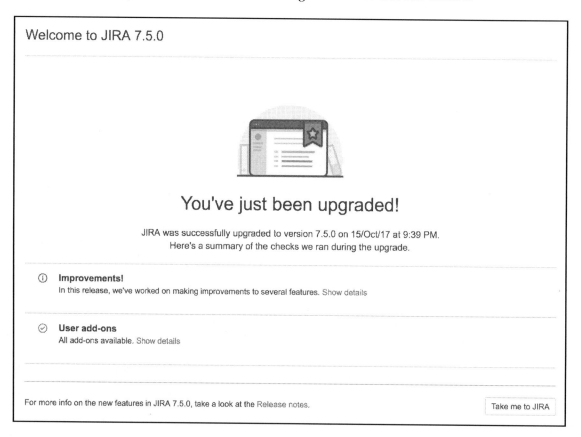

After clicking on the **Take me to JIRA** button, you will be automatically logged in with the administrator account you created earlier. Since this is the first time this account is being used, you will be asked to set up some personalization options, such as the preferred language and avatar. Once you have personalized the account, you will see the welcome screen, similar to the following screenshot:

Creating a sample project

Since we have just installed a fresh instance of Jira, we will be asked to create a new project. You have the option to import issues from existing data, such as a CSV file, or another issue-tracking system, such as Bugzilla, with the **Import issues** option. Create a new empty project and start using it right away with the **Create new project** option, or create a sample project with Jira's built-in sample data to explore and experiment with using the **Create sample project** option, which is what we will be doing in the following steps:

1. Click on the **Create sample project** button.
2. Select the type of project from the project template menu. We will be using the **Scrum software development** template:

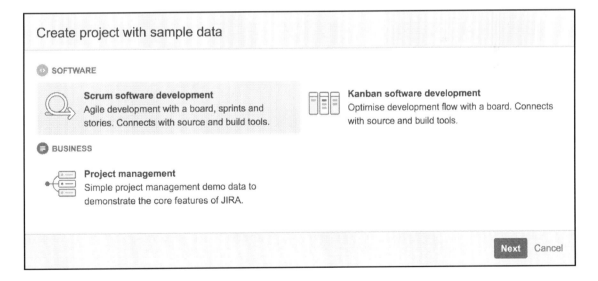

3. Enter a **Name** and **Key** for the new project:

4. Jira will create a new project and populate it with sample issues, and you will be taken to the new project and its agile board, which is a Scrum board in our case. We will talk about boards in the next section and the Scrum board in `Chapter 2,` *Jira Software for Scrum*.

Understanding Jira and its agile features

If you have used Jira before, especially prior to Jira 7, you would likely have used Jira for a variety of purposes, including—but not limited to—agile software development. In fact, before Jira 7, to have agile capabilities in Jira, you would have needed to install a separate add-on from Atlassian, called *Jira Agile*. Starting with Jira 7, agile features are bundled with the Jira Software product package, and you will not need any additional add-ons. There are, however, a number of useful third-party add-ons that can greatly enhance your experience, which we will cover in later chapters.

Since we will be focusing primarily on using Jira Software for agile software development purposes in this book, let's start with some agile concepts and look at how they are represented and used in Jira.

Agile board

The **agile board**, or simply board, is the main user interface that you, as the end user, will be using on a day-to-day basis for your projects. The agile board allows you to visualize tasks in a project and the available steps in the workflow, and gives you an interactive way to transition tasks through the workflow. Depending on the type of board you are using, there are also additional features that will provide a range of functionalities—for example, some may allow you to manage a backlog of features, provide visual cues to highlight potential bottlenecks, and more. Together with additional add-ons, you can even take snapshots of your agile board and place them onto a physical whiteboard, and vice versa. The following screenshot shows a sample Scrum board in work or sprint mode:

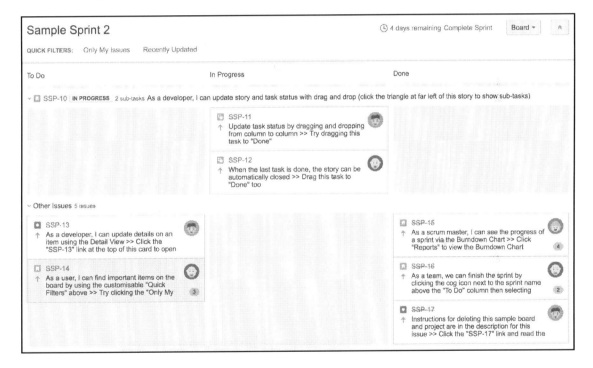

Card

A card is like a Post-it note that you might use on your whiteboard. It captures the user's story and represents the requirement or feature that is to be implemented. In Jira, each card represents a task or issue. The following screenshot shows what a card looks like on an agile board:

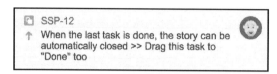

Issues and issue types

Every unit of work in Jira, such as a story or an epic, is uniformly referred to as an **issue**. Each issue has a field called **issue type**, which represents the type and purpose of the issue. For example, in a Scrum project, we would have the following issue types by default:

- **Epic**: This represents a big user story that has not been broken down into finer-grained requirements. In Jira, epics are usually used to define the "theme" for several stories that will be part of it, as well as modules or major components in a big development project.
- **Story**: This represents a single feature to be implemented. It is usually used to capture requirements from the end user's perspective. For this reason, stories are often written in nontechnical language and focusing on the desired results of the feature.
- **Bug**: This represents a defect or problem that needs to be fixed in the product.
- **Task**: This represents a generic task that is not a bug or a story, but which needs to be completed.

As we will see in later chapters, you can customize the list of issue types for your project to adapt to your project requirements better.

Fields

Each issue is made up of a number of fields, such as the issue type field mentioned earlier and other fields, such as summary, description, and assignee. Jira comes with a default set of fields to help you get started quickly, but as we will see in Chapter 5, *Customizing Jira Software*, it is very straightforward to add fields to your projects.

Workflows

Workflow is at the heart of Jira and is what powers Jira and its agile board in the background. As we will see in later chapters, Jira is able to integrate with your existing workflows, or adapt to and model after your development process. When you are just getting started, you do not have to know much about workflow as Jira will take care of it for you. We will cover workflows in more detail in Chapter 5, *Customizing Jira Software*.

Filters and JQL

The Jira agile board is able to work on either one specific project or multiple projects at once. When you want to have multiple projects, you will need to use filters to define what issues will be included. For this reason, understanding and being able to use **Jira Query Language (JQL)** effectively can be very handy. You can find more information on JQL at https://confluence.atlassian.com/jiracoreserver075/advanced-searching-935563511.html.

Using Jira agile project templates for agile

As we have already seen when creating our sample project, Jira comes with a number of project templates, such as Scrum and Kanban. Project templates let you create new projects based on predefined settings so that when the project is created, it will have all the necessary configurations set for you, including:

- **Issue type scheme**: An issue type scheme that contains only the relevant issue types for the selected template, such as stories and epics for Scrum.
- **Workflow**: A specially designed workflow, making it easier to work with yours issues on the agile board.
- **Screens**: A set of screens that contain the necessary fields for working with agile, such as epic links to link stories to epics, and sprint for when tasks are added to Scrum sprints.
- **Agile board**: An agile board that is dedicated to the new project, if the template is either Scrum or Kanban.

As we will see in later chapters, you can create agile boards for any existing projects, even if they are not created as Scrum or Kanban templates. These project templates are simply tools to help you get started quickly.

Summary

In this chapter, we looked at some of the basics of Jira Software and its support for agile methodologies. We installed an instance of Jira Software from scratch and created a project using the Scrum project template with sample data, which we will use in later chapters.

Now that we have laid out the basics of Jira Software, we will start to explore how we can use it to run agile projects, starting with the Scrum methodology in the next chapter.

2
Jira Software for Scrum

Scrum is one of the agile methodologies supported by Jira Software. Unlike the old days, when a single project manager would use either a spreadsheet or Microsoft Project to keep track of a project's progress, with Jira Software and Scrum, team participation is encouraged to improve collaboration between different project stakeholders. In this chapter, we will look at how we can use Jira Software to unlock the power of Scrum.

By the end of the chapter, you will have learned about the following topics:

- An overview of Scrum
- Setting up a Scrum board
- Managing an issue backlog
- Estimating work and team velocities
- Running the Scrum sprint
- Tracking and reviewing sprint progress

Scrum

Unlike the traditional waterfall methodology, where every task or project phase is sequential, Scrum prescribes the notion of iteration. At a high level, with Scrum, a project is broken up into a number of iterations called sprints. Each sprint is usually one or two weeks long. The project team completes a portion of the overall project, and the project is completed when all the sprints are finished. With this approach, the project team is able to do the following:

- Continuously deliver with each sprint so that feedback can be gathered early
- Accommodate changes during the project life cycle

- Identify issues early on rather than at the very end, which is costly
- Continuously improve the process with retrospective meetings at the end of each sprint

Roles in Scrum

In any Scrum team, there are three primary roles. Although each role has its own specific functions and responsibilities, you need all three to work together as a cohesive team in order to be successful at Scrum.

The product owner

The product owner is usually the product or project manager who is responsible for owning the overall vision and the direction of the product that the team is working on. As the product owner, they are in charge of the features that will be added to the backlog list, the priority of each feature, and planning the delivery of these features through sprints. Essentially, the product owner is the person who makes sure that the team is delivering the most value for the stakeholders in each sprint.

The Scrum master

The Scrum master's job is to make sure that the team is running and using Scrum effectively and efficiently, so they should be very knowledgeable and experienced in using Scrum. The Scrum master has the following two primary responsibilities:

- To coach and help everyone on the team to understand Scrum; this includes the product owner and delivery team, as well as external people that the project team interacts with. In the role of a coach, the Scrum master may help the product owner to understand and better manage the backlog and plan for sprints, as well as explain the process to the delivery team.
- To improve the team's Scrum process by removing any obstacles in the way. Obstacles, also known as **impediments**, are anything that may block or negatively affect the team's adoption of Scrum. These can include things such as a poorly organized product backlog or the lack of support from other teams/management. It is the responsibility of the Scrum master either remove to these impediments directly, or work with the team to find a solution.

Overall, the Scrum master is the advocate for Scrum, responsible for educating, facilitating, and helping people adopt and realize the advantages of using it.

The delivery team

The delivery team is primarily responsible for executing and delivering the final product. However, the team is also responsible for providing estimates on tasks and assisting the product owner in better planning sprints and delivery.

Ideally, the team should consist of cross-functional members required for the project, such as developers, testers, and business analysts. Since each sprint can be viewed as a mini project by itself, it is critical to have all the necessary resources available at all times, as tasks are being worked on and passed along the workflow.

Last but not least, the team is also responsible for retrospectively reviewing their performance at the end of each sprint, along with the product owner and Scrum master. This helps the team review what they have done and reveals how they can improve on their performance for the upcoming sprints.

Understanding the Scrum process

Now, we will give you a brief introduction to Scrum and an overview of the various roles that Scrum prescribes. Let's take a look at how a typical project is run with Scrum and some of the key activities.

First, we have the backlog, which is a one-dimensional list of the features and requirements that need to be implemented by the team. The item's backlogs are listed from top to bottom by priority. While the product owner is the person in charge of the backlog, defining the priority based on their vision, everyone in the team can contribute by adding new items to the backlog, discussing priorities, and estimating efforts required for implementation.

The team will then start planning their next immediate sprint. During this sprint planning meeting, the team will decide on the scope of the sprint. Usually, top-priority items from the backlog will be included. The key here is that by the end of the sprint, the team should have produced a fully tested, potentially shippable product containing all the committed features.

During the sprint, the team will have daily Scrum meetings, usually at the start of each day, where every member of the team will give a quick overview of what they have done, plan to do, and any impediments they may have encountered. The goal is to make sure that everyone is on the same page, so meetings should be short and sweet.

At the end of the sprint, the team will have a sprint review meeting, where the team will present what they have produced to the stakeholder. During this meeting, new changes will often emerge as the product starts to take shape, and these changes will be added to the backlog, which the team will reprioritize before the next sprint commences.

Another meeting called the sprint retrospective meeting will also take place at the end of the sprint, where the team will come together to discuss what they have done right, what they have done wrong, and how they can improve.

Throughout this process, the Scrum master will act as the referee, where they will make sure all these activities are done correctly. For example, the Scrum master will guide the product owner and the team during the backlog and sprint planning meetings to make sure the items they have are scoped and described correctly. The Scrum master will also ensure that the meetings stay focused, productive, do not run over time, and that the team members remain respectful without trying to talk over each other.

So, now you have seen some of the advantages of using Scrum and the different roles, as well as a simple Scrum process. Let's see how we can use Jira Software to run projects with Scrum.

Creating a new Scrum board

The first step to start using Jira Software for Scrum is to create a Scrum board for your project. If you created your project by using the Scrum project template, as shown in Chapter 1, *Jira Software Basics*, a Scrum board is automatically created for you, along with the project.

However, if you want to create a board for existing projects, or if you want your board to span across multiple projects, you will need to create it separately. To create a new board, perform the following steps:

1. Click on the **Boards** menu item from the top navigation bar and select the **View all boards** option.
2. Click on the **Create board** button. This will bring up the **Create an Agile board** dialog.
3. Select the **Create a Scrum board** option, as shown in the following screenshot:

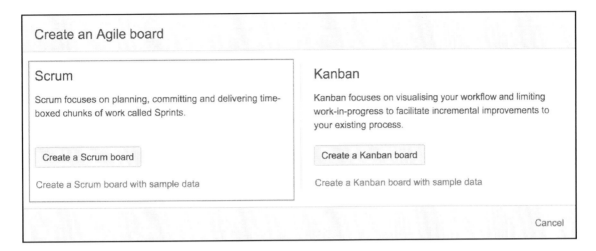

4. Select the way you want to create your board. There are three options to choose from, as follows:

- **Board created with new Software project**: This is the same as creating a project using the Scrum project template. A new project will be created, along with a new Scrum board dedicated to the project. Use this option if you want to create a new Scrum project from scratch.
- **Board from an existing project**: This option allows you to create a board that can span across multiple existing projects. Use this option if you have an existing project and would like to add a new Scrum board to it.
- **Board from an existing Saved Filter**: This option is similar to the existing project option, but lets you use a filter to define which issues will be included. Use this option if you want to create a board for multiple projects and have finer control over which issues to include.

If you have many issues in your project, you can also use filters to limit the number of issues to be included.

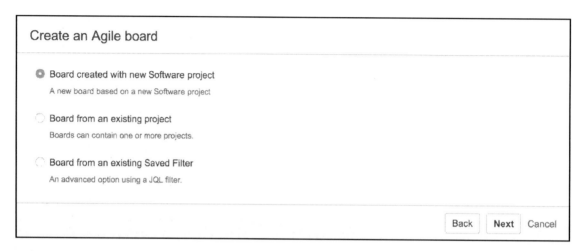

5. Fill in the required information for the board. Depending on the option you have selected, you will either need to provide the project details or select a filter to use. The following screenshot shows an example of how to create a board from two existing projects. Click on the **Create board** button to finish:

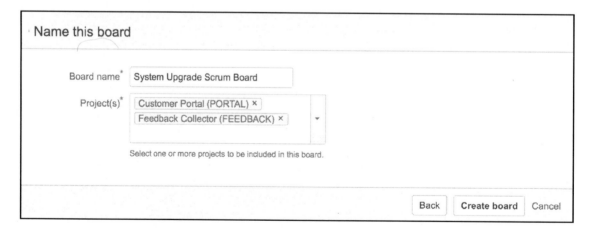

Understanding the Scrum board

The Scrum board is what you and your team will be using to plan and run your project. It is both your backlog as well as your sprint activity board. A Scrum board has the following major modes:

- **Backlog**: The **Backlog** mode is where you will plan your sprints, organize your backlog, and create issues.
- **Active sprints**: The **Active sprints** mode is where your team will be working in a sprint.
- **Releases**: The **Releases** mode shows you all the versions (see the later section in this chapter) you have for the project, and the progress for each.
- **Reports**: The **Reports** mode is where you can track the progress of your sprint.
- **Issues**: The **Issues** mode is the search mode, where you can search for issues in the project with a variety of filter options and advanced search queries.
- **Components**: The **Components** mode lists all the components in the project. With Scrum, epics are often used instead of components.

The following screenshot shows a typical Scrum board in the **Backlog** mode. In the center of the page, you have the backlog, listing all the issues. You can drag them up and down to reorder their priorities. On the right-hand side, you have the issue details panel, which will be displayed when you click on an issue in the backlog:

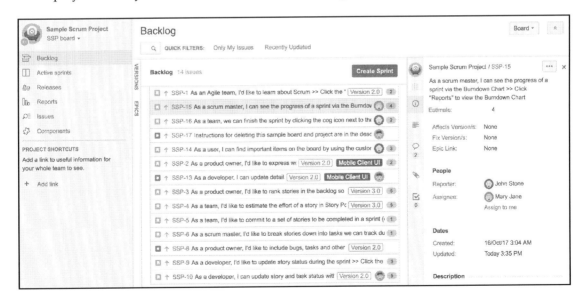

During the backlog planning meetings, the product owner and the team will use this **Backlog** mode to add new items to the backlog, as well as decide on their priorities.

Creating new issues

When a Scrum board is first created, all the issues, if any (also known as user stories, or stories for short), are placed in the backlog. During your sprint planning meetings, you can create more issues and add them to the backlog as you translate requirements into user stories. To create a new issue, perform the following steps:

1. Browse to your Scrum board.
2. Click on the **Create button** from the navigation bar at the top or press *C* on your keyboard. This will bring up the **Create Issue** dialog.
3. Select the type of issue (for example, **Story**) you want to create from the **Issue Type** field.
4. Provide additional information for the issue, such as **Summary** and **Description**.
5. Click on the **Create** button to create the issue, as shown in the following screenshot:

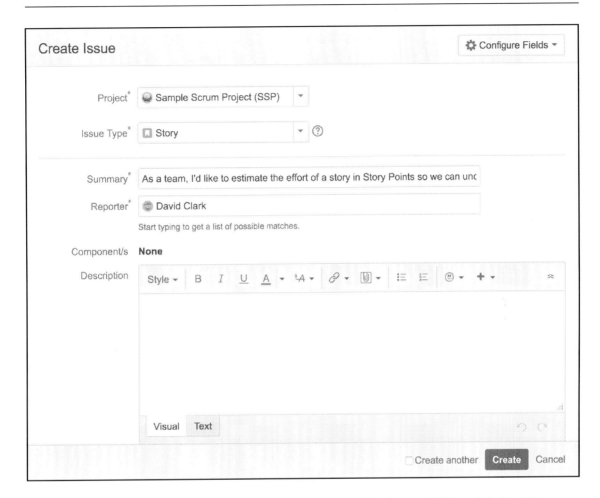

 The **Create Issue** screen can be customized to have additional fields. We will look at field and screen customization in `Chapter 5`, *Customizing Jira Software*.

Once you have created the issue, it will be added to the backlog. You can then assign it to epics or version and schedule it to be completed by adding it to sprints.

When creating and refining your user stories, you will want to break them down as much as possible so that when it comes to deciding on the scope of a sprint, it will be much easier for the team to provide an estimate. One approach is by using the **INVEST** characteristics defined by Bill Wake:

- **Independent**: It is preferable if each story can be done independently. While this is not always possible, independent tasks make implementation easier.
- **Negotiable**: The developers and product owners need to work together so that both parties are fully aware of what the story entails.
- **Valuable**: The story needs to provide value to the customer.
- **Estimable**: If a story is too big or complicated for the development team to provide an estimate, then it needs to be broken down further.
- **Small**: Each story needs to be small, often addressing a single feature that will fit into a single sprint (roughly 2 weeks).
- **Testable**: The story needs to describe the expected end result so that after it is implemented it can be verified.

Creating new epics

Epics are big user stories, or a big piece of work that would often need to be broken down into smaller, more manageable user stories. For example, an epic might be called Performance Improvement, which would contain numerous user stories, such as diagnosing performance problems and implementing various fixes. Epics can be, but are not required to be, completed in a single sprint, and they are usually delivered through several sprints, in the same order that the user stories they contain are prioritized. In Jira Software, epics are issues with the issue type set to Epic.

To create a new epic from your Scrum board, perform the following steps:

1. Expand the **EPICS** panel, if it is hidden, by clicking on **EPICS** from the left-hand side panel.
2. Click on the **Create Epic** link from the **EPICS** panel. The link will appear when you hover your mouse over the panel. This will bring up the **Create Epic** dialog, with the **Project** and **Issue Type** fields already preselected for you:

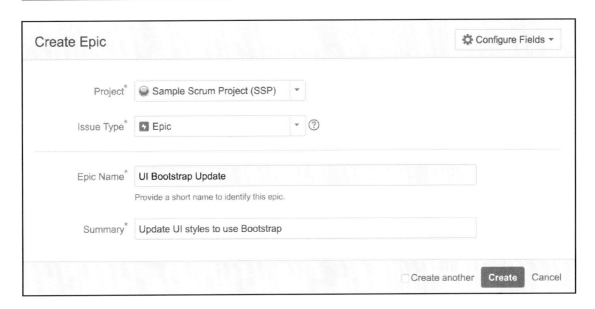

 You can also open the **Create Issue** dialog, as shown in the previous section, and select the **Issue Type** as **Epic**.

3. Provide a name for the epic in the **Epic Name** field.
4. Provide a quick summary in the **Summary** field.
5. Click on the **Create** button.

Once you have created the epic, it will be added to the **Epics** panel.

 Epics do not show up as cards in sprints or in the backlog.

After you have created your epic, you can start adding issues under it. Doing this helps you organize issues that are related to the same functionality or feature.

There are two ways in which you can add issues to an epic:

1. By creating new issues directly in the epic, expanding the epic you want, and clicking on the **Create issue in epic** link
2. By dragging existing issues into the epic, as shown in the following screenshot:

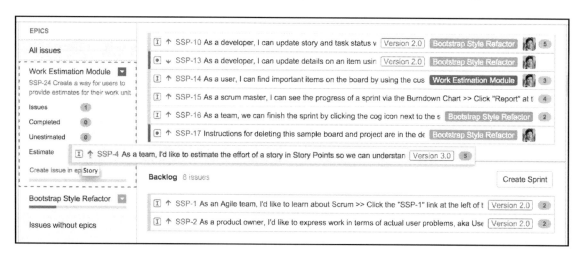

Estimating your work

Estimation is an art and is a big part of Scrum. Being able to estimate well as a team will directly impact how successful your sprints will be. When it comes to Scrum, estimation means velocity, or, in other words, how much work your team can deliver in a sprint. This is different from the traditional idea of measuring and estimating by man-hours.

The concept of measuring velocity is based around decoupling estimation from time tracking. So, instead of estimating the work based on how many hours it will take to complete a story, which will inadvertently make people work long hours trying to keep the estimates accurate, it can be easily done by using an arbitrary number for measurement, which will help us avoid this pitfall.

A common approach is to use what are known as story points. Story points are used to measure the complexity or level of effort required to complete a story, not how long it will take to complete it. For example, a complex story may have eight story points, while a simpler story will have only two. This does not mean that the complex story will take 8 hours to complete. It is simply a way to measure its complexity in relation to others.

After you have estimated all your issues with story points, you need to figure out how many story points your team can deliver in a sprint. Of course, you will not know this for your first sprint, so you will have to estimate this again. Let's say your team is able to deliver 10 story points worth of work in a one-week sprint. Then you can create sprints with any number of issues that add up to 10 story points. As your team starts working on the sprint, you will likely find that the estimate of 10 story points is too much or not enough, so you will need to adjust this for your second sprint. Remember that the goal here is not to get it right the first time, but to continuously improve your estimates to a point where the team can consistently deliver the same amount of story points' worth of work—that is, your team's velocity. Once you accurately start predicting your team's velocity, it will become easier to manage the workload for each sprint.

Now that you know how estimates work in Scrum, let's look at how Jira Software lets you estimate work.

Jira Software provides several ways for you to estimate issues, and the default approach is to use story points. Each story in your backlog has a field called **Estimate**, as shown in the following screenshot. To provide an estimate for the story, you just need to hover over the field, click on it, and enter the story point value:

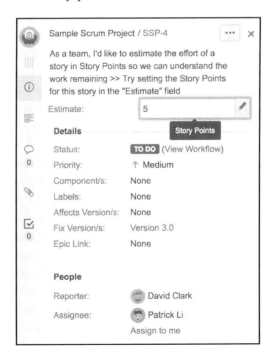

Consistency is the most important thing when it comes to estimates. It is better to be consistently wrong than inconsistently right and wrong. Of course, the goal is to go from being consistently wrong and improve to become consistently right.

Remember that the estimate value you provide here is arbitrary, as long as it can reflect the issues' complexity in relation to each other. Here are a few more points for estimation:

- Be consistent in how you estimate issues.
- Involve the team during estimation.
- If the estimates turn out to be incorrect, that is fine. The goal here is to improve and adjust.

Ranking and prioritizing your issues

During the planning session, it is important to rank your issues so that the list reflects their importance relative to each other. For those who are familiar with Jira, there is a priority field, but since it allows you to have more than one issue sharing the same priority value, it becomes confusing when you have two issues both marked as critical.

With Scrum, you should prioritize issues by dragging an issue up and down the list according to its importance. This is usually done when you are grooming your backlog. By having the most important issues at the top of the backlog, when it comes to sprint planning, you can easily add issues to your sprint by dragging the sprint footer, as we will see later.

Creating new versions

In a software development team, you will likely be using versions to plan your releases. Using versions allows you to plan and organize issues in your backlog and schedule when they will be completed. You can create multiple versions and plan your roadmap accordingly.

To create a new version, follow these steps:

1. Expand the **Versions** panel, if it is hidden, by clicking on **VERSIONS** from the left-hand side panel.

2. Click on the **Create Version** link from the **Versions** panel. The link will appear when you hover your mouse over the panel. This will bring up the **Create Version** dialog with the **Project** field preselected for you, as shown in the following screenshot:

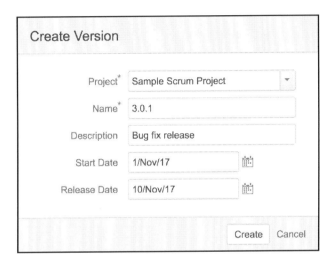

3. Provide a name for the version in the **Name** field.

4. You can also specify the start and release dates for the version. These fields are optional, and you can change them later.

5. Click on the **Create** button.

Once the version is created, it will be added to the **Versions** panel. Just like epics, you can add issues to a version by dragging and dropping the issue over onto the target version. In Scrum, a version can span across many sprints. Clicking on a version will display the issues that are part of the version. As shown in the following screenshot, **Version 2.0** spans across three sprints:

Planning sprints

The sprint planning meeting is where the project team comes together at the start of each sprint and decides what they should focus and work on next. With Jira, you will be using the **Backlog** mode of your board to create and plan the new sprint's scope.

Now we illustrate some of the key components during sprint planning:

- **Backlog**: This includes all the issues that are not in any sprint yet. In other words, it includes the issues that are not yet scheduled for completion. For a new board, all existing issues will be placed in the backlog.

- **Sprints**: These are displayed above the backlog. You can have multiple sprints and plan ahead.
- **Issue details**: This is the panel on the right-hand side. It displays details of the issue you are clicking on.
- **Epics**: This is one of the panels on the left-hand side. It displays all the epics you have.
- **Versions**: This is the other panel on the left-hand side. It displays all the versions you have.

The highlighted area in the following screenshot is the new sprint, and the issues inside the sprint are what the team has committed to deliver at the end of the sprint:

Starting a sprint

Once all the epics and issues have been created, it is time to start preparing a sprint. The first step is to create a new sprint by clicking on the **Create Sprint** button.

There are three ways to add issues to a sprint:

- By dragging the issues you want from the backlog and dropping them into the sprint.
- By editing the issues' sprint fields and selecting the sprint you want to add the issues to.
- By dragging the sprint footer down to include all the issues from the backlog that you want to be part of the sprint. This is a quick way if you have groomed your backlog so that the issues you want to focus on are at the top.

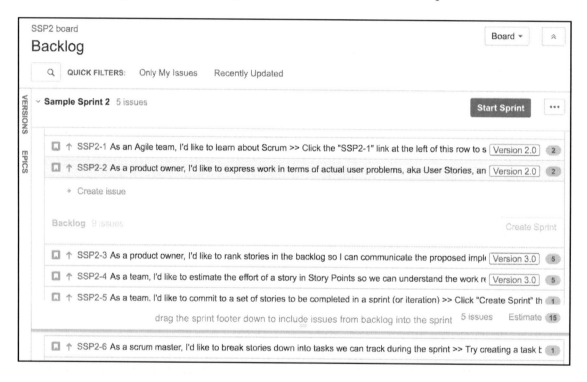

You can create multiple sprints and plan beyond the current one by filling each sprint with issues from your backlog.

Once you have all the issues you want in the sprint, click on the **Start Sprint** button. As shown in the following screenshot, you will be asked to set the start and end dates of the sprint. By default, Jira will automatically set the start date to the current date and the end date to one week after that. You can change these dates, of course. The general best practices include the following:

- Keeping your sprints short, usually one or two weeks long.
- Keeping the length of your sprints consistent; this way, you will be able to predict your team's velocity accurately:

Once you have started your sprint, you will be taken to the **Active Sprints** mode for the board.

Note that for you to start a sprint, you have to take the following things into consideration:

- There must be no sprint already active. You can only have one active sprint per board at any time. There is, however, an option that allows you to run parallel sprints, which we will talk about in the next section.
- You must have the **Administer Projects** permission for all projects included in the board. We will cover permissions in Chapter 5, *Customizing Jira Software.*

Running parallel sprints

By default, you can only have one active sprint at one time. However, sometimes you may have multiple teams working on the same project, but in unrelated areas. In these cases, you may want to have multiple sprints running for the project, one for each team. You can enable parallel sprints using the following method:

1. Log into Jira as an administrator, such as the user we created during installation.
2. Browse to the **Applications** section of the administration console.
3. Select the **Jira Software configuration** option from the left panel.
4. Check the **Parallel Sprints** option to enable it.

Once this option is enabled, you will be able to start multiple sprints in the same project. Note that this is a global option, so all projects will be allowed to have parallel sprints.

Working on a sprint

You will enter the Active Sprints mode once you have started a sprint; all the issues that are part of the sprint will then be displayed. In the Active Sprints mode, the board will be divided into two major sections.

The main section will contain all the issues in the current sprint. You will notice that it is divided into several columns. These columns represent the various states or statuses that an issue can be in, and they should reflect your team's workflow. By default, there are three columns:

- **To Do**: The issue is waiting to start
- **In Progress**: The issue is currently being worked on
- **Done**: The issue has been completed

As we will see in the next chapter, you can customize these columns by mapping them to Jira workflow statuses.

If you are using epics to organize your issues, this section will also be divided into several horizontal swimlanes. Swimlanes help you group similar issues together on the board. Swimlanes group issues by criteria, such as assignee, story, or epic. By default, swimlanes are grouped by stories.

So, you can see that columns group issues by statuses, while swimlanes group issues by similarity. As shown in the following screenshot, we have three columns and two swimlanes:

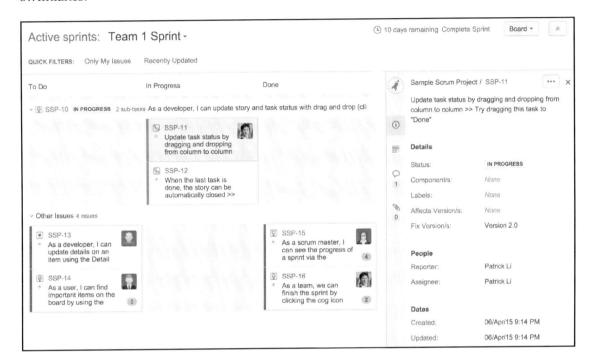

Both the swimlanes and workflow columns can be customized to suit the way your team works best, and we will cover this in Chapter 4, *Using Jira Software Your Way.*

The second section will appear on the right-hand side after you have clicked on an issue, and it will display the issue's details, such as its summary and description, comments, and attachments.

In a typical scenario, at the start of a sprint, all the issues will be in the left-most **To Do** column. During the daily Scrum meetings, team members will review the current status of the board and decide what to focus on for the day. For example, each member of the team may take on an issue and move it to the **In Progress** column by simply dragging and dropping the issue cards into the column. Once they have finished working on the issues, they can drag them into the **Done** column. The team will continue this cycle throughout the sprint until all the issues are completed:

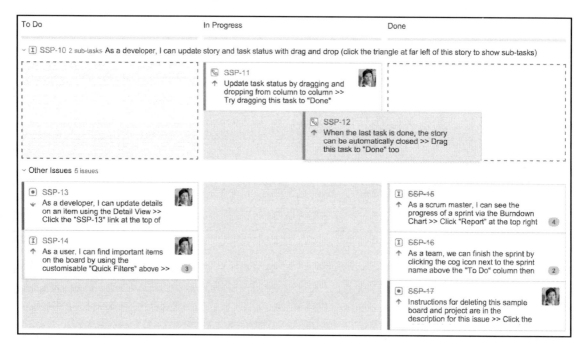

During the sprint, the Scrum master, as well as the product owner, will need to make sure that they do not interrupt the team unless it is urgent. The Scrum master should also assist with removing impediments that are preventing team members from completing their assigned tasks.

The product owner should also ensure that no additional stories are added to the sprint and that any new feature requests are added to the backlog for future sprints instead. Jira will alert you if you try to add a new issue to the currently active sprint.

Completing a sprint

On the day the sprint ends, you will need to complete the sprint by performing the following steps:

1. Go to your Scrum board and click on **Active Sprints**.
2. Click on the **Complete Sprint** link. This will bring up the **Complete Sprint** dialog, summarizing the current status of the sprint. As shown in the following screenshot, we have a total of six issues in this sprint. Three issues are completed and three are not:

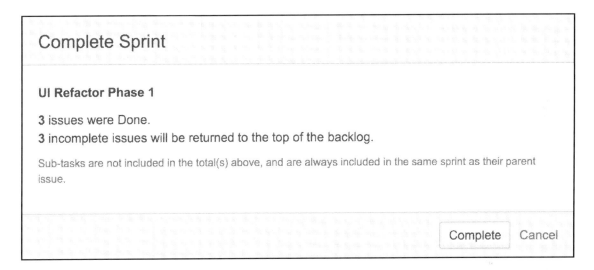

3. Click on the **Complete** button to complete the sprint.

When you complete a sprint, any unfinished issues will be automatically moved back to the top of the backlog. Sometimes, it might be tempting to extend your sprint if you only have one or two issues outstanding, but you should not do this. Remember that the goal here is not to make your estimates appear accurate by extending sprints or to force your team to work harder in order to complete everything. You want to get to a point where the team is consistently completing the same amount of work in each sprint. If you have leftovers from a sprint, it means that your team's velocity should be lowered. Therefore, for the next sprint, you should plan to include less work.

Reporting a sprint's progress

As your team busily works through the issues in the sprint, you need to have a way to track the progress. Jira provides a number of useful reports via the **Report** mode. You can access the **Report** mode anytime during the sprint. These reports are also very useful during sprint retrospective meetings as they provide detailed insights on how the sprint progressed.

The sprint report

The sprint report gives you a quick snapshot of how the sprint is progressing. It includes a burndown chart (see the next section) and a summary table that lists all the issues in the sprint and their statuses, as shown here:

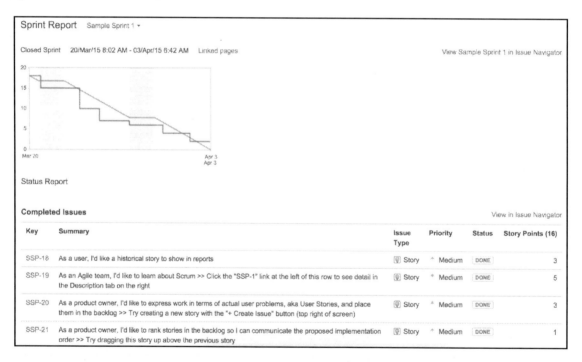

As shown in the preceding sprint report, we have completed six issues in the sprint. One issue was not completed and was placed back in the backlog.

The burndown chart

The burndown chart shows you a graphical representation of the estimated or ideal work that is left to be done versus the actual progress. The gray line acts as a guideline for the projected progress of the project and the red line is the actual progress. In an ideal world, both lines should be as close to each other as possible as the sprint progresses each day:

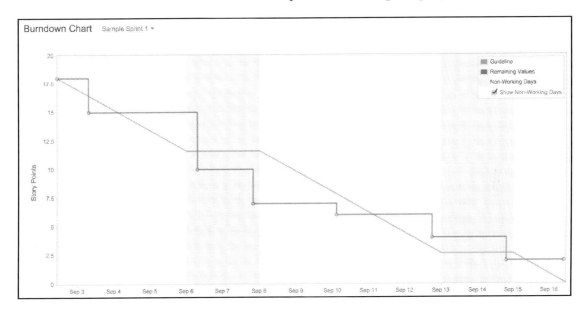

The velocity chart

The velocity chart shows you the amount of work originally committed to the sprint (the gray bar) versus the actual amount of work completed (the green bar) based on how you decide to estimate, such as in the case of story points.

The chart will include past sprints, so you can get an idea of the trend and be able to predict the team's velocity. As shown in the following screenshot, from sprints 1 to 3, we have overcommitted the amount of work, and for **Sprint 4**, we have completed all our committed work. So, one way to work out your team's velocity is to calculate the average based on the **Completed** column, and this should give you an indication of your team's true velocity.

Of course, this requires:

- That your sprints stay consistent in their duration
- That your team members stay consistent in their efficiency
- That your estimation stays consistent in its formulation

As your team starts using Scrum, you can expect to see improvements to the team's velocity as you continuously refine your process. Over time, you will get to a point where the team's velocity becomes consistent and can be used as a reliable indicator for work estimation. This will allow you to avoid over- and under committing to work delivery, as shown in the following velocity chart:

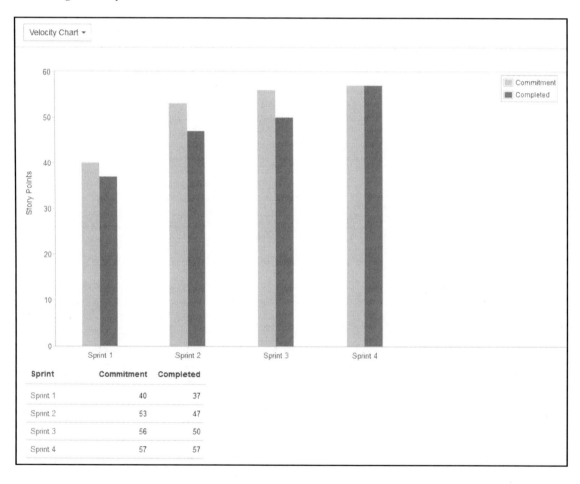

Summary

In this chapter, we looked at how to use Jira for Scrum. We looked at the Scrum board and how you can use it to organize your issue backlog, plan and run your sprint, and review and track its progress with reports and charts. Remember that the key elements to focus on for a successfully running sprint are consistency, review, and continuous improvement. It is fine if you find your estimates are incorrect, especially for the first few sprints; just make sure that you review, adjust, and improve.

Now that you have seen how to use a Scrum board, in the next chapter, we will look at how you can use Jira for Kanban.

3
Jira Software for Kanban

In the last two chapters, we have looked at how to use Jira Software for the Scrum agile methodology. Jira Software also supports another agile methodology called Kanban, which many agile teams have chosen to use instead of Scrum. In this chapter, we will look at how to use Jira Software for Kanban.

By the end of this chapter, you will have learned how to:

- Visualize workflow with Kanban
- Work on issues the Kanban way
- Customize your Kanban board
- Create reports and charts for improvements

Kanban

Kanban is another agile methodology that is supported by Jira Software. Unlike Scrum (which was introduced in `Chapter 2`, *Jira Software for Scrum*), which revolves around the notion of running your project in planned iterations called sprints, Kanban does not run in iterations, or rather, the use of iteration is optional with Kanban.

In a nutshell, Kanban has the following three concepts:

- **Visualizing workflow**: This breaks down your tasks (issues) and puts them on the board. You need to organize your board so that each column represents a status in your overall workflow, ordered from left (start) to right (finish).
- **Limiting the work in progress (WIP)**: This sets minimum and maximum limits for how many tasks can be in any given workflow status.
- **Measuring the lead time**: This calculates the average time required to complete one task, keeping it as low and predictable as possible.

While Scrum requires the team to plan iterative sprints with managed scopes, and focuses on team velocity, Kanban is more flexible, as its focus is more around **cycle time**. Cycle time is the measurement of the amount of time it takes for an issue, or unit of work, to transition through the team's workflow from end to end. The goal is to reduce the cycle time, identify any problems and bottlenecks in the workflow, and address them to get the process to flow smoothly again. As we will see, Jira provides a number of tools to help with this.

Creating a new Kanban board

Jira Software provides a simple-to-follow wizard to help you create new Kanban boards. All you need to do is choose if you want to create a board from scratch, from an existing project, or filter, and follow the steps.

To create a new Kanban board, perform the following steps:

1. Click on the **Agile** menu from the top navigation bar and select the **Manage Boards** option.
2. Click on the **Create board** button. This will bring up the **Create an Agile board** dialog.
3. Select the **Create a Kanban board** option:

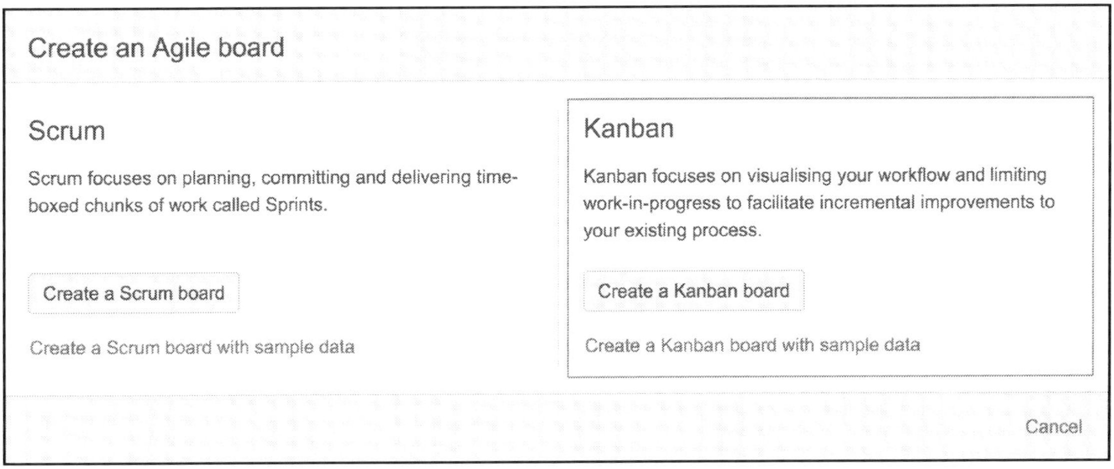

Create an Agile board

Scrum

Scrum focuses on planning, committing and delivering time-boxed chunks of work called Sprints.

Create a Scrum board

Create a Scrum board with sample data

Kanban

Kanban focuses on visualising your workflow and limiting work-in-progress to facilitate incremental improvements to your existing process.

Create a Kanban board

Create a Kanban board with sample data

Cancel

4. Select how you want to create your board and click on the **Next** button. There are three options to choose from to create your board, as shown in the screenshot below. These options are explained as follows:

- **Board created with new Software project**: This is the same as creating a project using the Scrum agile project template. A new project will be created, along with a new Kanban board dedicated to the project.
- **Board from an existing project**: This option allows you to create a new board from your existing projects. The board will be dedicated to only one project.
- **Board from an existing Saved Filter**: This option allows you to create a board that can span across multiple projects with the use of a filter. So, to use this option, you will first have to create a filter that includes the projects and issues you need.

If you have many issues in your project, then you can also use filters to limit the number of issues that are to be included.

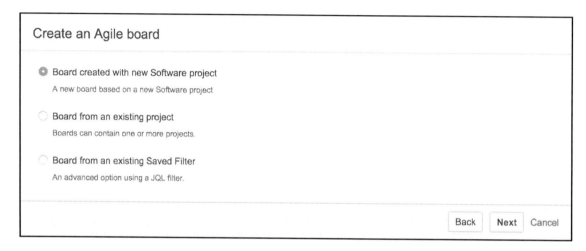

5. Fill in the required information for the board. Depending on the option you have selected, you will either need to provide the project details or select a filter to use. The following screenshot shows an example of creating a board with a filter. Click on the **Create board** button to finish:

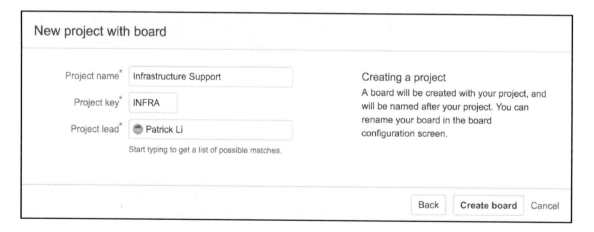

Understanding the Kanban board

For those who are familiar with the Scrum board in Jira Software, the Kanban board will look very similar to the work mode of the Scrum board, with only a few differences:

- There is no backlog view. The backlog is the first column on the board—new issues will be added straight into the **Backlog** column.
- There are no active sprints. Since Kanban does not have iterations, you are always in the working view.
- Some of the columns may have a minimum and maximum number, which appear next to the column name.
- Some of the columns may be highlighted in red or yellow, as shown in the following screenshot, where the **In Progress** column is highlighted in red:

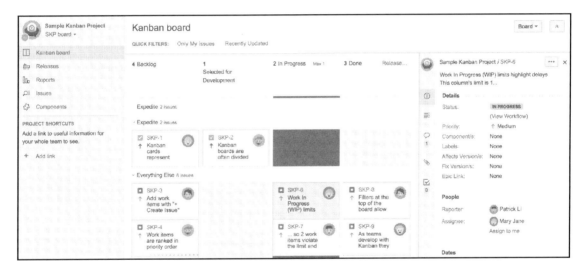

So, let's take a closer look at the Kanban board and see why we have these differences. First of all, as explained in the earlier section, Kanban does not use discrete time periods, such as iterations, to plan work in advance. Instead, work is being done constantly, going from the backlog to the finish line to be released. Therefore, the Kanban board does not have separate views for the backlog (or a **Plan** mode, in older versions of Jira Software) and the current active sprints (or **Work** mode); everything is combined into this single Kanban board view, which shows you everything in your backlog and the current progress as your team works through the issues.

The first column on the board will be your backlog, and it is called **Backlog** by default if you are not using a customized board and/or workflow. Any new issues created will be automatically placed into that column. However, if you have a big project, you may find this hard to maintain as the number of issues grows. In this case, Jira provides an option to have a backlog view like a Scrum board by using what is known as **Kanplan**. We will cover Kanplan in Chapter 4, *Using Jira Software Your Way*.

Customizing your Kanban board

After you have created your Kanban board, you will need to customize it based on your workflow process and your team's capacity. Some of the key customizations include:

- Modeling your board columns to mimic your workflow
- Setting minimum and maximum constraints for your workflow status so as to control the work in progress
- Controlling which issues will be included and displayed on the board
- Categorizing issues on the Kanban board in swimlanes
- Creating custom-filtered views with quick filters

Visualizing workflow with Kanban

One of the core concepts of Kanban is to visualize the team's workflow to better understand what the team is currently working on, what the workload is like, and where in the workflow a given task is. So the first step is to set up your board columns to visually represent what your workflow looks like.

In Jira, workflow statuses are represented as columns on the Kanban board. To customize your Kanban board's columns, perform the following steps:

1. Go to the Kanban board you want to customize.
2. Click on the **Board** drop-down menu and select the **Configure** option.
3. Select **Columns** from the left-hand navigation menu.
4. Click on the **Add column** button.
5. Enter a name for the new column and select a category for it. Generally speaking, if the column represents the start of the workflow, then it should be in the **To Do** category. If it represents the end, then it should be in the **Done** category. Otherwise, use the **In Progress** category.
6. Click on the **Add** button to create the new column:

Once you have created the new column, it will be added as the second to last column on the list. You can rearrange its position by dragging the column left or right on the list so that it is in the correct position in your workflow.

 When adding a column this way, a corresponding new status with the same name will also be created for you, if one does not already exist. So you do not have to create both the column and status separately.

Generally speaking, your board should reflect how work progresses through your workflow, so you should have a column for each major step that members of your team will be working on. For example, if you have the steps **In Development**, **Development Completed**, and **In Testing** in your workflow, you should have two columns, one for **In Development** and one for **In Testing**. The reason why you should not have a column for **Development Completed** is because nobody will be working on the issues that are in the step.

Setting up column constraints

As stated earlier, one of the key differences between Scrum and Kanban is that Scrum limits the amount of work per iteration and Kanban limits the amount of work per workflow status. This is done by setting **column constraints**. Column constraints tell Jira the maximum and/or the minimum number of issues that should be in a column at any given time.

To set up column constraints, perform the following steps:

1. Go to the Kanban board you want to customize.
2. Click on the **Board** drop-down menu and select the **Configure** option.
3. Select **Columns** from the left-hand navigation menu.
4. Choose how you want the column constraint to be calculated from the **Column Constraint** field. If you select the **None** option, column constraints will not be applied to this board.
5. Set the minimum and maximum constraint value for the status in its corresponding columns. For example, as shown in the following screenshot, for the **Selected for Development** column, the team should have a minimum of five issues, and no more than ten issues in the status:

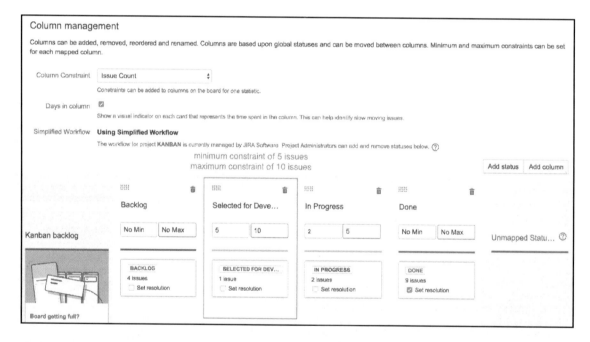

Once you have set the minimum and maximum constraints for workflow statuses, the Kanban board will let you know if those constraints are violated. For example, as shown in the following screenshot, we only have one issue in the **Selected for Development** status, which has a minimum constraint of five issues, and so the column is highlighted in yellow.

We also have six issues in the **In Progress** status, which has a maximum constraint of five issues, so the column is highlighted in red:

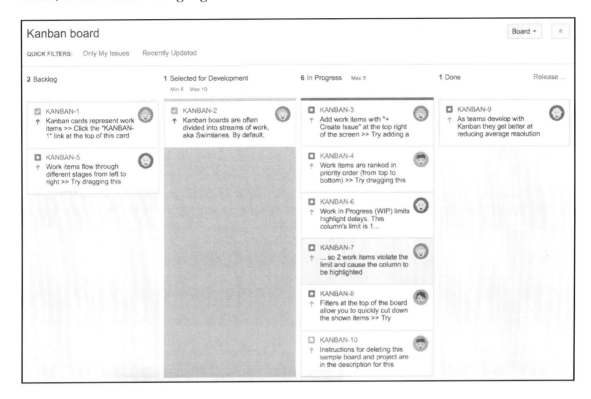

When you start seeing these constraint violations, it means the team should start reassessing the current workload. Remember, the goal with Kanban is to help you identify and improve efficiency, not get in the way of your work.

Column constraints help you to identify bottlenecks and inefficiencies in your workflow, not to restrict your work process.

Controlling which issues to show on the board

For the Kanban board, there are two queries used to determine which issues will be displayed:

- **Saved Filter**: The saved filter includes issues that will be displayed on the Kanban board. The **Filter Query** field shows the JQL query of the saved filter. Depending on how the board is created, the saved filter will be either automatically created or selected from an existing filter list.
- **Kanban board sub-filter**: The sub-filter determines which issues from the saved filter will be considered unreleased. As we will see in a later section in this chapter, *Releasing a version in Kanban,* once an issue is released as part of a new version, it is removed from the board.

As shown in the following screenshot, **Sample Kanban Board** is using the **Filter for Sample Kanban Project** saved filter with the JQL query of `project="SampleKanbanProject"ORDERBYRankASC`. This means that all issues created in **Sample Kanban Project** will be shown on the board. It is also using the JQL query of `fixVersioninunreleasedVersions()ORfixVersionisEMPTY`, which means issues that have an unreleased version as their fix versions, or do not have a value for the field, will be considered unreleased and will be displayed on the board:

General and filter

The Board filter determines which issues appear on the board. It can be based on one or more projects, or custom JQL depending on your needs.

General

Board name	**Sample Kanban Project**
Administrators	**Patrick Li (patrick)**

Filter

Saved Filter	**Filter for Sample Kanban Project**
	Edit Filter Query
Shares	🔒 **Project:** Sample Kanban Project
	Edit Filter Shares
Filter Query	**project = SKP ORDER BY Rank ASC**
Ranking	**Using Rank**
Kanban board sub-filter	**fixVersion in unreleasedVersions() OR fixVersion is EMPTY**
	Further filtering of issues for unreleased work.

You can change both the saved filter and sub-filter used for your board. If you want to simply use a different saved filter for another filter you have, perform the following steps:

1. Hover over and click on the saved filter's name. You will see it change to a select list.
2. Select the new saved filter from the list. If you do not see the filter you want, you can type in the filter's name and search for it. Note that you can only see and select filters that you have access to.

You can also change the JQL query of the saved filter currently in use:

1. Click on the **Edit Filter Query** link under **Saved Filter**. This will bring you to **Issue Navigator**, the interface where you create and edit filters in Jira, as shown in the following screenshot:

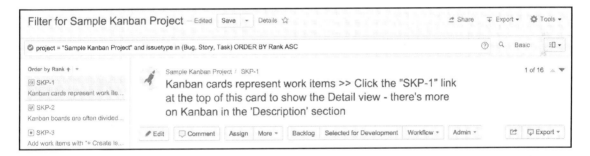

2. Update your search filter criteria via the UI controls if you are in the **Basic** mode, or the JQL query directly if you are in the **Advanced** mode.
3. Click on the **Save** button at the top to update your filter.

As shown in the preceding example, we changed our filter's query to `project="SampleKanbanProject"andissuetypein(Bug,Story,Task)ORDERBYRankA SC`, which limits the issues to types of bugs, stories, and tasks only.

To update the board's sub-filter to customize how unreleased issues are determined, follow these steps:

1. Hover over and click on the Kanban board sub-filter's content. You will see it change to an editable text box.
2. Enter the new JQL query and click on the **Update** button, as follows:

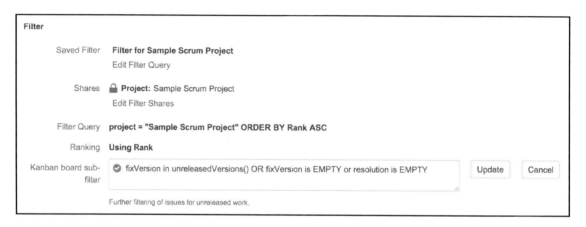

As shown in the preceding example, we have changed the sub-filter's query to `fixVersioninunreleasedVersions()ORfixVersionisEMPTYorresolutionisEMPTY` t o also include a check for issues that do not have a value for the **Resolution** field.

Organizing your Kanban board with swimlanes

Swimlanes are a useful way to group and organize your issues on your Kanban board. For example, you can use swimlanes to represent priorities and divide issues based on owners or types.

By default, when you first create a new Kanban board, you will have two swimlanes, but you can also create your own custom ones. For example, as shown in the following screenshot, we have three swimlanes: the **Expedite** and the **Everything Else** swimlanes are created along with your board, and the **Bugs** swimlane in the middle is a custom swimlane we have added:

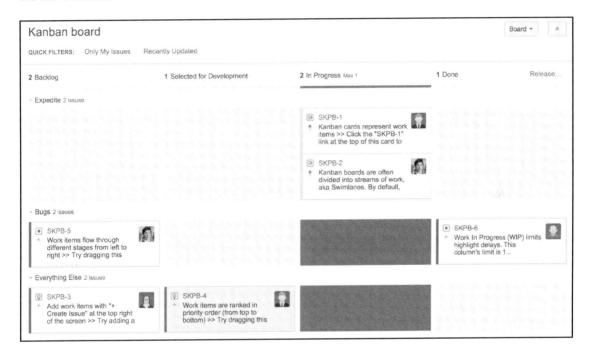

To customize swimlanes for your Kanban board, perform the following steps:

1. Go to the Kanban board that you want to customize swimlanes for.
2. Click on the **Board** drop-down menu and select the **Configure** option.
3. Select **Swimlanes** from the left-hand navigation menu.
4. Choose the criteria you want to base your swimlane on in the **Base Swimlane on** field.

5. Create a new swimlane by entering the name and description for the swimlane and enter the JQL query if you are basing your swimlanes on queries.
6. Reorder your swimlanes by dragging them up and down the list:

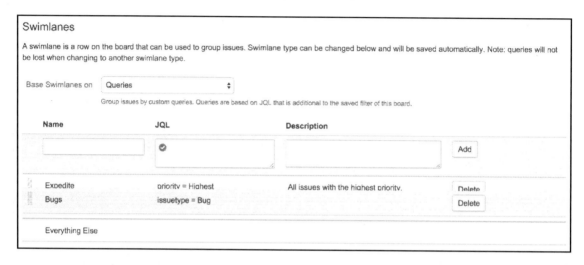

As shown in the preceding screenshot, we have three swimlanes based on queries. The **Expedite** and **Everything Else** swimlanes were there by default when we created the board. We have a new **Bugs** swimlane that is using the JQL query of `issuetype=Bug` so that all issues of the **Bug** type will be categorized together.

Note that the order of the swimlanes is important. The order will determine both the placement of each swimlane and the swimlane that an issue will belong to. In this case, the **Expedite** swimlane is on the top, and this will be reflected in the final Kanban board. If we have an issue that is of the **Bug** type and also a value of **Highest** for the **priority** field, it will be categorized into the **Expedite** swimlane rather than the **Bugs** swimlane because of the order.

The JQL option is the most flexible way of defining swimlanes, but you can also use some of the built-in options, such as **Assignee**, for simpler purposes. The next screenshot shows a Kanban board with four swimlanes, each showing the issues for a user, so you can easily get an idea of how many issues are assigned to each user:

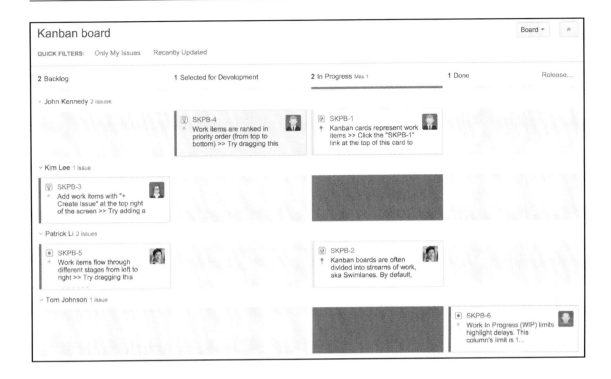

Creating custom views with quick filters

By default, the Kanban board will display all the issues that are returned from the selected filter. However, there might be times where you need to do additional filtering on top to narrow down the list of issues further. This is where quick filters come in.

Quick filters let you define additional filtering based on JQL. This is like creating a custom view for the board to include only the issues that you are interested in seeing for the time being. To create new quick filters, perform the following steps:

1. Go to the Kanban board you want to add quick filters to.
2. Click on the **Board** drop-down menu and select the **Configure** option.
3. Select **Quick Filters** from the left-hand navigation menu.
4. Enter a name and description for the new quick filter.
5. Enter the JQL query for the filter. Jira Software will help you construct and validate the query.

6. Click on the **Add** button to create the new quick filter:

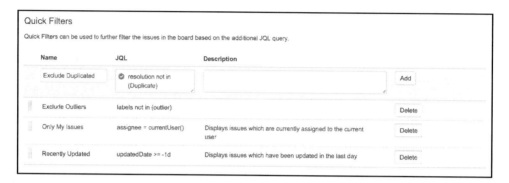

As shown in the preceding screenshot, we have three quick filters already created, and we are creating a new one named **Exclude Duplicated** with the JQL query of `resolutionnotin(Duplicate)` to remove all issues with the value of **Duplicate** in the resolution field from the board.

Once you have created the new quick filters, they will be displayed above the issue cards, as shown in the following screenshot:

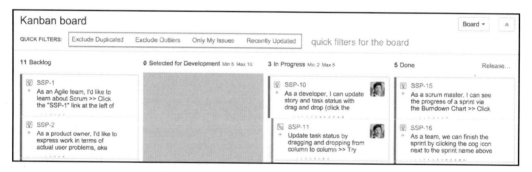

Releasing a version in Kanban

With Kanban, tasks are not assigned to a predefined or planned release schedule, which is different to Scrum, where releases usually happen at the end of a sprint. When using Kanban, releases are made at the team's discretion as more and more tasks are being completed. The idea here is to continuously release new features and improvements as and when it makes sense for the team.

For example, some teams may choose to release on a regular basis, such as every Friday. Other teams may choose to release only when they have completed something useful.

To release a version from your Kanban board, perform the following steps:

1. Click on the **Release...** link at the top right-hand corner of your board.
2. Enter the version number from the **Release** dialog.
3. Select the release date.
4. Enter a short description for the version.
5. Click on the **Release** button to release the version, as shown in the following screenshot:

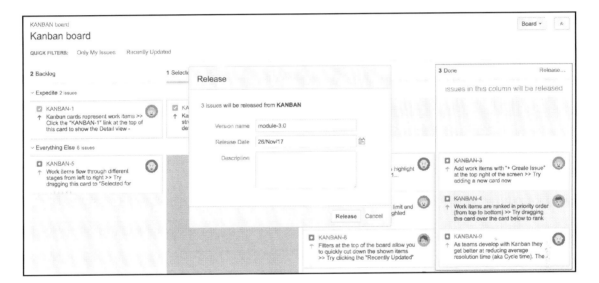

 You must have the **Administer Projects** permission for all projects included in the board in order to release the version. We will cover permissions in `Chapter 5`, *Customizing Jira Software*.

Once you have released a version, all the issues in the last column will have the version number added to their **Fix Versions** field, and will be taken off the Kanban board.

One thing to note about versions when working in Kanban is that you should not create the version you want to release ahead of time.

It is important to note that with Kanban, the release plan is to be continuously optimized. There is no point in releasing something simply because of a rule that states a release needs to be made on a Friday, when there are not many completed tasks. The team needs to look at their current lead time and then make the decision as to whether or not it makes sense to make a release.

Improving your team's performance

One common question that often pops up when teams are starting with Kanban is, *what is the correct limit I should set for each of my workflow statuses?* The answer is simple: try and experiment.

The first step is to look at your board and see if any constraints are being violated. If we take a look at the following example of a Kanban board, we can see that too many issues are in the **In Progress** column, and at the same time, we don't have enough issues in the **QA** column. What this tells us is that we have a bottleneck in our development phase of the workflow. This results in work being piled up in development while the QA engineers are waiting around and not being productive:

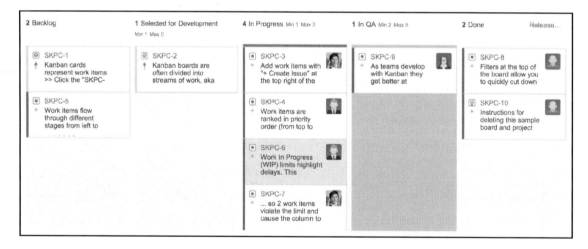

So in order to address this, as a team you will need to take a close look at the bottleneck—in this case, the **In Progress** column—and figure out why this is happening. For example, perhaps you do not have enough developers to handle the workload and people are multitasking in order to try to complete as much work as possible. This will often cause unnecessary context switching, which in turn causes inefficiency, or perhaps the tasks are too complicated and need to be broken down.

Defining the column constraint can be an art, and once you have set the constraints, you will need to periodically review them and refine them as the project and team changes. When setting column constraints, keep the following points in mind about the limits you choose:

- **Limit set too high**: You will have idle tasks sitting around, and this will lead to bad lead/cycle time.
- **Limit set too low**: You will have idle people waiting for work, and this will lead to bad productivity.

Remember, with Kanban, you and your team should continuously improve your process; the board helps you to highlight any potential bottlenecks, so you and your team can improve your processes.

Do not just fix the board—fix the cause of the bottleneck.

Improving the process with charts and reports

Jira Software comes with a number of useful charts and reports to help you visualize your team's performance and identify potential bottlenecks in your Kanban process. To generate a report, perform the following steps:

1. Browse to the Kanban board you want to generate a report on.
2. Click on the **Reports** tab from the left-hand panel of your board.

As shown in the following screenshot, there are a number of reports that are available. The reports under the **Agile** section are specifically designed for using agile methodologies, such as Kanban. Of course, the other reports, such as **Pie Chart Report**, are also very useful, but since these are vanilla Jira reports, we will be focusing mainly on the agile reports, namely **Cumulative Flow Diagram** and **Control Chart**:

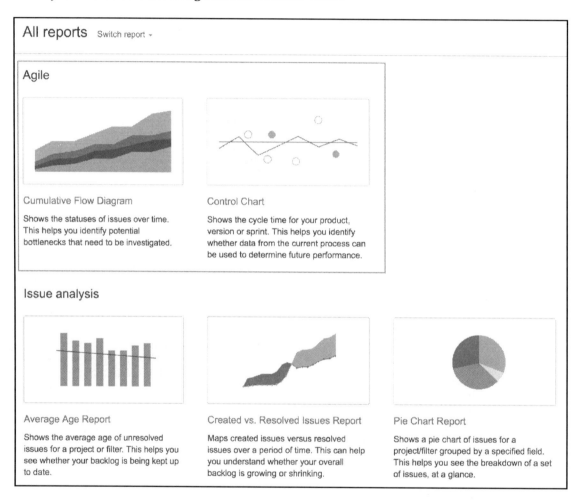

Since Kanban is a continuous process, you should run these reports regularly.

Cumulative flow diagram

The first useful chart Jira Software provides is the cumulative flow diagram. This chart shows you the number of issues (*y* axis) in various statuses, displayed as colored bands, over a period of time (*x* axis). This way, you will be able to visually identify whether there are any bottlenecks in a particular status in your team's workflow, as you will see a widening in the colored band representing the status.

To generate the cumulative flow diagram for your Kanban board, perform the following steps:

1. Click on the **Reports** tab from the left-hand panel of your board.
2. Select the **Cumulative Flow Diagram** option:

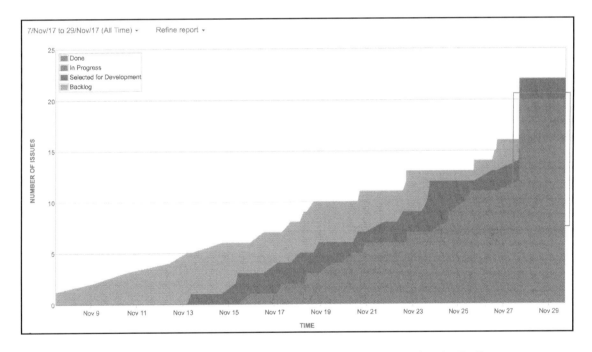

In the preceding sample chart, we can see there is a sudden surge for the **In Progress** status (represented as the purple band) toward the end of the month, around November 29. This indicates that there is a bottleneck, with issues getting stuck in the **In Progress** status, and it is worth investigating what is causing this.

With the cumulative flow diagram, you can hover over the diagram and see what issues are being moved into the various statuses so that you can get a clearer picture of what is happening. If your diagram gets a bit busy, you can refine it by selectively hiding statuses (columns), swimlanes, and issues (via quick filters) to display only the data you are interested in, as shown in the following screenshot:

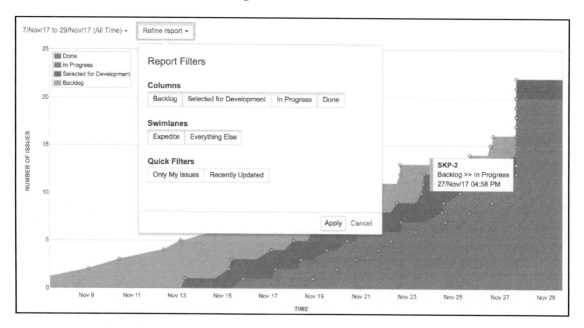

Control chart

The second useful chart to help you measure your team's performance is the control chart. The control chart shows you the average lead time of your team over a period of time, and plots the issues on the chart so you can see the following:

- Any issues that are outside of the standard deviation, also known as outliers
- The average time taken to complete tasks
- The team's rolling average and how it compares to the average

To generate the control chart for your Kanban board, perform the following steps:

1. Click on the **Reports** tab from the left-hand panel of your board.
2. Select the **Control Chart** option.

As shown in the following screenshot, the control chart shows:

- Issues on the board represented by green dots. A hollow green dot represents a single issue and a solid green dot (bigger) represents multiple issues. You can click on these dots to see the issue details.
- The time period is shown as dates on the x axis.
- The time it takes for issues to be completed on the y axis.
- The average duration for issue completions, shown as the red line.
- The average lead time for issues, shown as the blue line. A downward trending blue line indicates improvements in efficiency.
- The standard deviation, shown as a light-blue band:

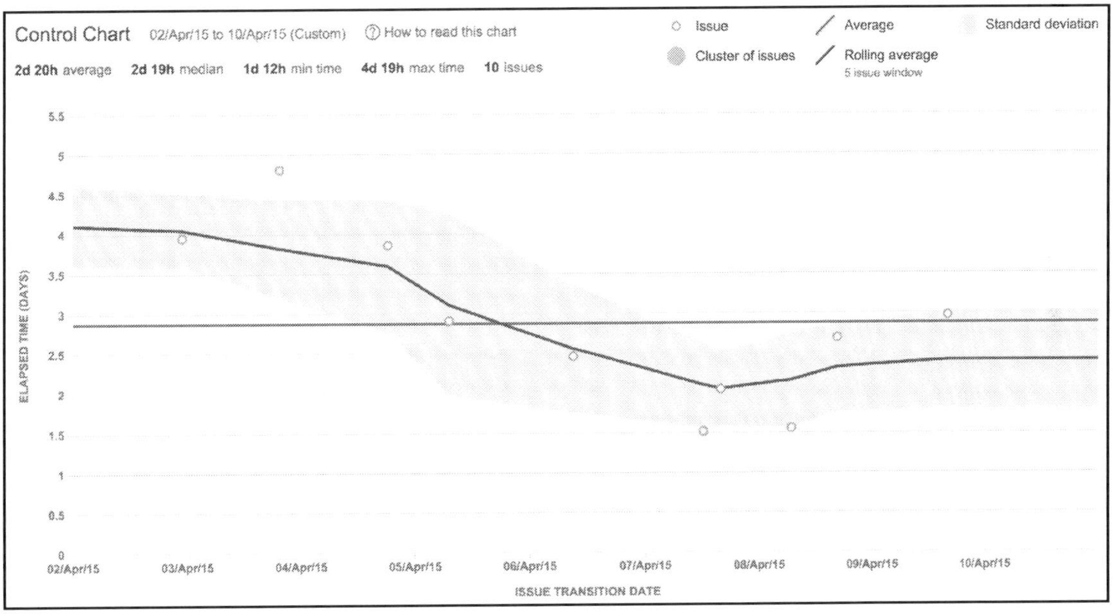

Generally, you would want to have the blue line trending downwards; this would indicate a decrease in the average lead time. This means that issues are not stuck in workflow statuses and are being completed quickly, and that your team is not overbooked.

You would also want to have a low standard deviation. This is an indication of how each issue is measured against the rolling average (blue line). The narrower the blue band, the closer each issue is being delivered to the average time. This means that it's more likely the team will be able to deliver work at the same rate.

Customizing the control chart

The control chart has several customization options that allow you to fine tune the data being displayed on the chart. These options are displayed below the chart itself, as shown in the following screenshot:

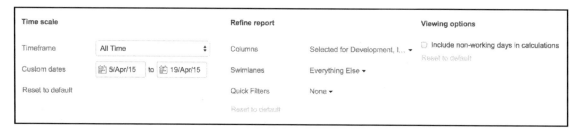

When you first start working with the control chart, you should want to identify and remove the outliers from the chart as they can often skew your data and give you incorrect readings.

Outliers are the green dots far above the light-blue band; these are often issues that are created or transitioned incorrectly because of human error. You can easily filter out these issues by applying a label to each of the issues and creating a new quick filter. To do this, perform the following steps:

1. Review each outlying issue and apply a label (outlier) to it if it is confirmed to be an outlier.
2. Create a new quick filter for the board with the following JQL:
   `labelsnotin(outlier)`.
3. Select the new quick filter from the **Quick Filters** field on the control chart.

You can use this technique to filter out other issues that might skew your chart, such as duplicated issues.

Summary

In this chapter, we looked at using Jira Software for Kanban. We have looked at the Kanban board and how to configure it to model your existing workflow, as well as setting up column constraints to limit the work in progress, which is the key concept with Kanban. We also looked at some of the charts that are available to help you identify potential bottlenecks in your process so that you and your team can work together to address those issues and improve your process.

Now that we have covered using Jira for both Scrum and Kanban, we will look at some of the unique additions Jira brings to these two agile methodologies, namely Scrumban and Kanplan, in the next chapter.

4
Using Jira Software Your Way

In the previous chapters, we looked at how to use Jira for both Scrum and Kanban agile methodologies. Jira comes with a set of tools to support these two methodologies, as well as sensible defaults to get you up and running quickly. However, you will often need to customize what comes out of the box by default in order to better suit your needs. In this chapter, we will go over some of the important options Jira Software provides so it can better adapt to the way you need to run your projects. We will also expand on some of the hybrid methodologies Jira Software offers, where you can combine the best of both Scrum and Kanban.

By the end of the chapter, you will have learned how to:

- Manage your Scrum board's configuration
- Control which issues are to be included on your board
- Customize your Scrum board's column layouts
- Use swimlanes to group your issues
- Filter issues on your Scrum board with quick filters
- Combine the power of Scrum and Kanban with Scrumban and Kanplan

Managing your board

When you first create an agile board using Jira's built-in templates for either Scrum or Kanban, as outlined in the previous chapters, the board is created with a set of default settings, and you as the person who created the board will be automatically set as the board's administrator.

As the administrator, you can further customize the agile board in many ways, including:

- Scope of the board—what projects/issues will be included on the board
- Permission of the board—who will have access to the board
- Layout of the board—the board's vertical columns and horizontal swimlanes
- Customized filters—additional ways to filter out contents on the board

First of all, to start customizing your agile board:

1. Go to the agile board you want to customize.
2. Click on the **Board** drop-down menu and select the **Configure** option.
3. Select **General** from the left-hand navigation menu. As you can see from the following screenshot, the INFRA board has two administrators set. You can add and remove administrators by simply hovering over the field and updating the values:

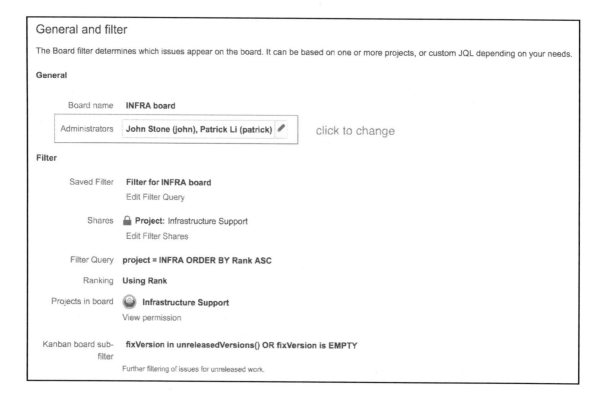

The following table provides a summary of the configuration fields:

Field	Description
Board name	Name of the agile board.
Administrators	Users who can configure the agile board's settings. You can add more administrators by either selecting the users directly or by selecting a group.
Saved Filter	This controls which issues will be included on the agile board. If you have created your board using the agile templates, then the filter here is automatically created for you to include all issues in the project. You can select a different filter to use or click on the **Edit Filter Query** link to change the current filter.
Shares	This controls who will have access to the filter. In practice, the filter should be shared with the same users who have access to the board.
Filter Query	This shows you the actual filter query used by **Saved Filter**.
Ranking	This shows whether ranking is currently enabled. You need to have ranking enabled to rank issues and create sprints.
Projects in board	Projects that are part of the board. This is automatically determined based on the **Saved Filter** used by the board.

Controlling board scope

When we talk about the scope of your agile board, we are referring to the issues that will be included on your board. If you have created your board while creating a new project or have taken it from an existing project, then the scope of your board will be the selected project, meaning all issues from the project will be available for the board to display.

The way Jira controls the scope of a board is by using what is called a **saved filter**. A saved filter is a search query that has been saved in the system, and the issues returned from the result of the query are the issues that will be included on the board. When you create a board from a project, a new saved filter is automatically created for you, with its query parameter set to the selected project. For example, as shown in the following screenshot, the **INFRA board** is created from the **Infrastructure Support** project, so Jira has automatically created a saved filter called **Filter for INFRA board** with the filter query set to `project = INFRA ORDER BY Rand ASC`.

This saved filter is effectively saying, *all issues with their project set to the project key INFRA will be included in this board, and they will be ordered by the Rank field in ascending order*:

 The **Saved Filter** is a standard Jira feature used in areas other than agile boards. It uses the **Jira Query Language (JQL)**. You can find out more about JQL at `https://confluence.atlassian.com/jiracoreserver073/ advanced-searching-861257209.html`.

You can change the scope of your board by either changing the actual saved filter's query by clicking the **Edit Filter Query** link, or by using a different saved filter. Note that in order for you to change the current saved filter's query; you need to have the required permission. So if you do not have permission, then your best option is to create a new saved filter and set your board to use that instead. We will cover filter permissions in the next section.

Managing board permissions

In the previous section, we learned that Jira uses saved filters to determine which issues will be included on an agile board. Now let us take a look at how to manage the access permissions of a board.

There are two key permission levels when it comes to accessing an agile board, illustrated as follows:

- Accessing the board itself—based on the saved filter
- Accessing the issues on the board—based on project permission

Access to an agile board is controlled by the permission set on the saved filter or who the filter is shared with. If a user has access to the filter, then the user will have access to the board. For a filter that is automatically created as part of the board, it is set to be shared with all members of the project. If you are the owner of the filter, you can click on the **Edit Filter Shares** link and then choose who to share the filter with, as shown in the following screenshot. For this particular filter, it is shared with all members of the `Sample Scrum Project`:

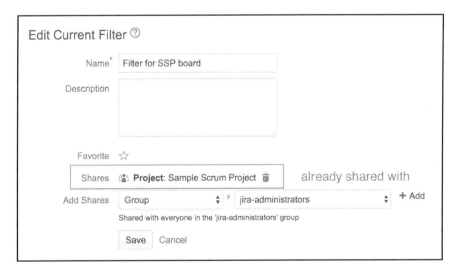

The saved filter determines access to the agile board, and then it is up to each of the project's permissions to determine whether a user should be allowed to view its issues. This means that if a user has access to a saved filter, but does not have the necessary permission to access the project, then the user will be looking at an empty board with no issues on it.

Since a saved filter can have more than one project, the agile board will list all the projects that are part of it in the **Project in board** section, and if you are an administrator of a project, you can click on the **View permission** link to review and update its permissions. We will be covering permissions in `Chapter 5`, *Customizing Jira Software* as it is a complicated topic. For now, suffice it to say that if a user is able to access an agile board, but is not able to view all its issues, then this is due to project permission settings.

Enabling ranking

Ranking allows you to prioritize your issues by dragging and dropping them into your backlog and sprints. The higher an issue is in the ranking, the more important it is. If ranking is disabled, you will get an error message similar to `Ranking is disabled, as the Filter Query for this board is not ordered by Rank`, when you try to drag your issues in the backlog.

If you have created your agile board by using the agile templates with either the new project or existing project option, then ranking will be enabled by default. However, if it is disabled for some reason, you can enable ranking by following these steps:

1. Go to the agile board you want to customize.
2. Click on the **Board** drop-down menu and select the **Configure** option.
3. Select **General** from the left-hand navigation menu.
4. Click on the **Add Rank** button at the bottom to enable ranking:

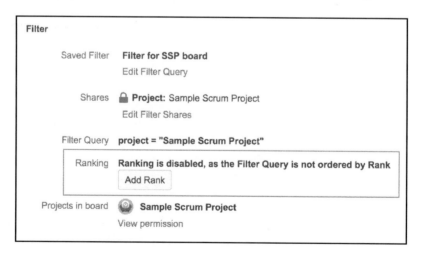

After you have enabled ranking, you will notice that your **Filter Query** value is automatically updated. So, in the preceding screenshot, the query `project = "Sample Scrum Project"` will be changed to `project = "Sample Scrum Project" ORDER BY Rank ASC`. Make sure you do not remove the `ORDER BY Rank ASC` part of the query, as that is the snippet that enables ranking for your query and board.

Customizing your board's layout

Jira's agile board acts as the white board where all your story cards are placed. There are two key components that make up the board, namely the columns and swimlanes:

- **Columns**: The vertical columns that are used to represent the state of a story card
- **Swimlanes**: The horizontal rows that help you to better categorize your story cards on the board

In the following sections, we will take a deeper look into these two components and how you, as the board administrator, can customize them to get the most out of your board.

Working with columns

Columns represent the statuses that an issue can be in. On a simple board, as shown in the following screenshot, we have three columns, and they are each mapped to an issue status:

- **To Do**: Issues that are waiting in the queue to be worked on are mapped to the **To Do** workflow status
- **In Progress**: Issues that are currently being worked on are mapped to the **In Progress** workflow status

- **Done**: Issues that are completed are mapped to the **Done** workflow status:

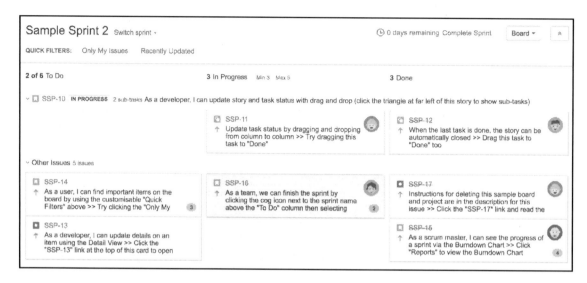

This is a very simple setup where issues only have three steps from start to finish. Often, you will have an existing workflow that is more complex than this.

Jira and workflow

Before we get into customizing columns, we first need to take a quick look at workflows in relation to Jira. As you may already know, Jira uses workflows to move an issue from one status to the next. Jira also leverages this feature by mapping its columns to workflow statuses. However, if you are not familiar with how workflow works in Jira, do not worry—we will cover workflows in detail in Chapter 5, *Customizing Jira Software*.

Since workflows in Jira can often get very complicated, it is sometimes difficult to use the traditional Jira workflows in an agile environment. So Jira introduced what is known as the **agile simplified workflow**.

Agile simplified workflow refers to workflows that are managed directly from within Jira that are simplified and streamlined for agile usage.

This allows you to:

- Maintain your workflow from your agile board, managed as board columns
- Move issues freely from one status (column) to another without restrictions from workflow conditions and validators
- Not have intermediate screens where you move issues between statuses, making it much easier to move cards (issues) on your boards
- Automatically set resolution values (as per your definition) when issues are moved to appropriate statuses (columns)

If you have created your agile board by using the built-in agile templates, then you are most likely using an agile simplified workflow.

Creating new columns

If you are the board administrator, you can customize the board's columns to better reflect your workflow:

1. Navigate to the Scrum board that you want to customize.
2. Click on the **Board** drop-down menu and select the **Configure** option.
3. Select **Columns** from the left-hand navigation menu.

From the **Column management** page, you can customize the following options:

- **Columns**: You can add, remove, and rename columns.
- **Column Layout**: You can rearrange the order of columns.
- **Issue Status Mapping**: You can map columns to issue statuses. For each column, you can have one or more issue statuses mapped to it.
- **Column Constraint**: You can add constraints to columns, limiting how many issues can be in a status at any given time.

Let's start with creating new columns. There are two ways new columns can be created and mapped to issue statuses, depending on whether you are using an agile simplified workflow or not.

You can determine whether you are using the simplified workflow by looking at the **Simplified Workflow** field, and seeing if it says **Using Agile Simplified Workflow**, as shown in the following screenshot:

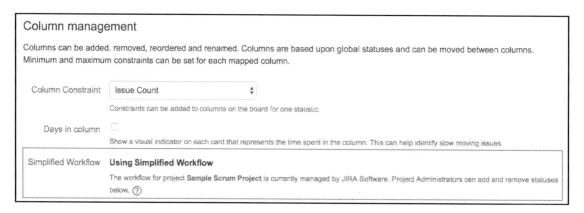

For a new column to be usable, it needs to have at least one status mapped. If you are using the agile simplified workflow, this is a very straightforward process. The agile simplified workflow takes care of this for you, so you don't have to worry about manual column status mapping. It is recommended that you use the agile simplified workflow where possible. To add a new column, perform the following steps:

1. Click on the **Add column** button. A new column will be added to the list in the penultimate position.
2. Enter a name and select a category for the new column. A new issue status with the same name will also be created and mapped to the new column. Generally speaking, if the new column is going to be the first column on the board, select **To Do** as the category. If it is going to be the last column, select the **Done** category. Otherwise, select the **In Progress** category.

If you are not using the agile simplified workflow, you will need to perform the following steps:

1. Create the new column as outlined in the preceding list.
2. Create new workflow statuses to be mapped to the new column and add the statuses used by the workflow.
3. Manually drag and drop the statuses into the new column, as shown in the following screenshot:

You can also map additional statuses to columns by dragging the statuses you want to map from under the **Unmapped Statuses** section and dropping them into the target column. Once you have mapped at least one status to the new column, it will be displayed on the board in active sprint mode.

It is recommended that you have one column per workflow status to keep the flow logical and simple. However, you can have multiple statuses mapped to one column, as shown in the preceding screenshot. As you can see, we have both the **Done** and **Fixed** statuses mapped to the **Done** column. You will usually find the need to do this if you are creating a Scrum board for an existing project with a workflow in place, or if you have a complex workflow that cannot be mapped to columns on the board one to one. When you map multiple statuses to a column, such as the **Done** column in our example, and move an issue into the column, you will be able to select the appropriate status, as shown in the following screenshot:

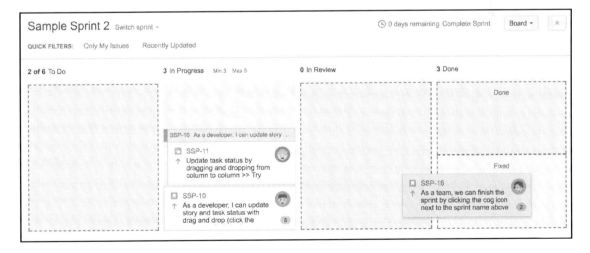

When using the agile simplified workflow, you will see a checkbox option called **Set resolution** in the mapped workflow status. If you check this option, when an issue is moved into the corresponding column, it will be automatically assigned the resolution value of **Done**. Jira makes use of the resolution value to determine whether an issue is completed, so it is important to assign a value for the status/column that represents the end of the workflow.

If you are not using the agile simplified workflow, this option is not available; the resolution must be set using a workflow transition screen.

Setting up column layout

Once you have created all your new columns and mapped them to workflow statuses, you can rearrange the layout by dragging and dropping the columns left and right to their desired locations, as shown in the following screenshot. The order of your column should reflect your workflow, starting from the left and moving to the right so that it visually represents the logical flow of an issue through the work process:

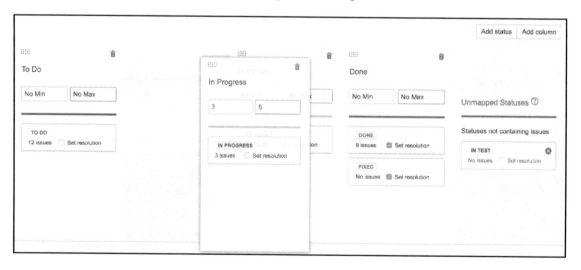

As we will see in `Chapter 6`, *Jira Software – Advanced*, you will be able to export your issues from your board onto a physical board and import them back in, as long as the column layout of your Jira agile board is the same as your physical board.

Working with swimlanes

Swimlanes are the horizontal counterparts to the columns on a board. Unlike columns, which are always mapped to issue statuses, you can base your swimlanes on several criteria:

- **Queries**: These are Jira search queries constructed with JQL. With this option, each swimlane will only show results from its own query. For example, you can create a query for each priority value, so you can group your issues based on their importance.
- **Stories**: Each swimlane will be mapped to a story. All subtasks that fall under the story will be displayed in the swimlane.
- **Assignees**: Each swimlane will be mapped based on the issue's assignee.
- **Epics**: Each swimlane will be mapped to an epic. All issues that fall under the epic will be displayed in the swimlane.
- **Projects**: Each swimlane will be mapped to a project. If there is only one project, there will be only one swimlane.

Using swimlanes is a great way to group and categorize your issues on your Scrum board. For example, with the **Assignees** option, you can easily get an idea of each team member's workload by just looking at the board.

The following screenshot shows a Scrum board with three swimlanes based on issue priority, using the queries option:

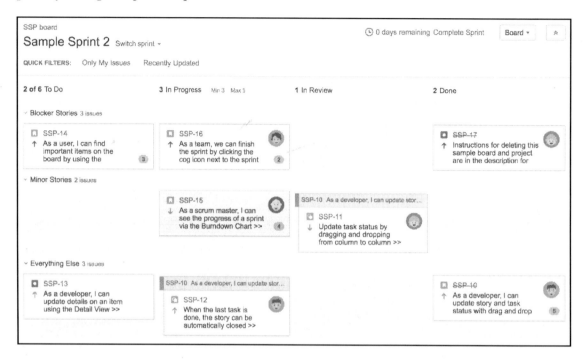

Setting up swimlanes

If you are the board administrator, you can customize the board's swimlanes to better organize your story cards:

1. Navigate to the Scrum board you want to customize.
2. Click on the **Board** drop-down menu and select the **Configure** option.
3. Select **Swimlane** from the left-hand navigation menu.
4. Choose the criteria you want to base your swimlanes on from the **Base Swimlanes on** field.

5. If you choose to base your swimlanes on **Queries**, you will need to enter the name for each swimlane and its corresponding JQL query, as shown in the following screenshot:

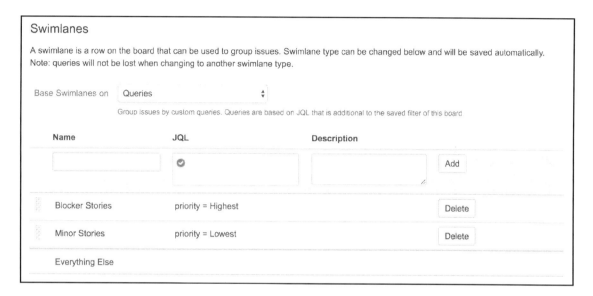

Using quick filters

When you have a big project team, your board can get very busy. Sometimes you want to narrow them down and focus on issues that fit specific criteria, such as bugs, or issues that are assigned to a specific user.

By using quick filters, we can remove the unnecessary *noise* by filtering out all the issues that do not fit the criteria, letting you focus on the issues that you care about, as shown in the following screenshot:

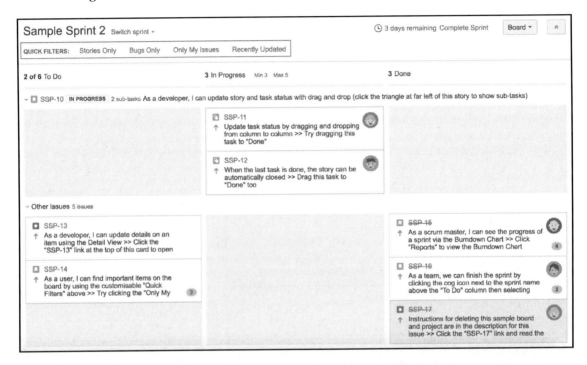

You can think of quick filters as additional views for your Scrum board. For example, the preceding screenshot shows four quick filters for the Scrum board: **Stories Only, Bugs Only, Only My Issues**, and **Recently Updated**. By using the **Bugs Only** quick filter, you can get a view of your board showing only bug issues. You can toggle a quick filter on and off by clicking on it. When turned on, it will be highlighted in blue and update the board with only issues that fit the filter's criteria. Clicking on the filter again will unapply it. You can have more than one quick filter applied to a board at the same time, and only issues that fit all the filters' criteria will be shown.

Creating new quick filters

All agile boards come with two default quick filters:

- **Only My Issues**: This displays issues that are assigned to the currently logged-in user
- **Recently Updated**: This displays issues that have been updated in the last 24 hours

If you are the board administrator, you can create new quick filters for your board to help you and your team to better visualize your issues. To do this, perform the following steps:

1. Navigate to the agile board that you want to customize.
2. Click on the **Board** drop-down menu and select the **Configure** option.
3. Select **Quick Filters** from the left-hand navigation menu.
4. Enter a name for the filter in the **Name** field. The name entered here will be displayed on the agile board.
5. Enter the search query for the filter in the **JQL** field, as shown in the following screenshot.
6. Click on the **Add** button to create the new filter.

Once created, the new quick filter will be available to everyone using the board:

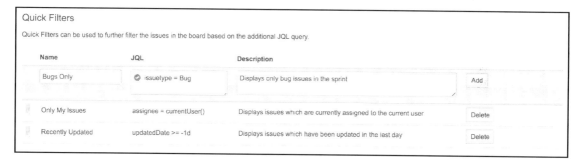

In our example, as shown in the preceding screenshot, the JQL query `issuetype = Bug` means that issues that have the value `Bug` for their issue type field will be included.

Scrumban

The first mixed agile methodology is called **Scrumban**. As you may have guessed from its name, it is a methodology based on Scrum, but with a hint of Kanban mixed in. As we have seen in Chapter 2, *Jira Software for Scrum*, the Scrum methodology revolves around grooming a backlog of tasks and running your project in iterations, called sprints. While this is a great way to plan and manage your project, it sometimes fall short when it comes to actually visualizing the execution of your sprints, which is something Kanban is great at. So instead of forcing you to make a choice between the two methodologies, Jira lets you use Scrum as the basis, so you can still run your project with time-boxed sprints and bring in some of the features and benefits of Kanban, and this hybrid methodology is called Scrumban.

In Chapter 3, *Jira Software for Kanban*, we introduced column constraints and how Jira uses that to visually show you bottlenecks in your workflow on a Kanban board. This same approach is also how Jira lets you use part of Kanban's features in Scrum. For example, we have set a constraint that there should be a minimum of three and no more than five issues in the **In Progress** column for our Scrum board, as shown in the following screenshot:

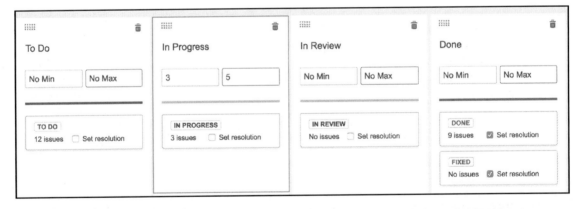

Just like with Kanban, once you have placed constraints on a column, if it is violated, the column will be highlighted. As shown in the following screenshot, the **In Progress** column has a maximum constraint of three issues, but we have four, so it is highlighted in red. The **In Review** column has a minimum constraint of two issues, but we have one, so it is highlighted in yellow:

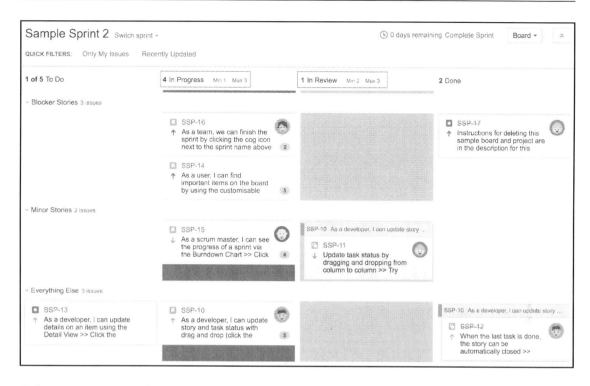

Column constraints do not prevent you from violating the limits. They simply help to flag areas where there might be a problem. Setting the limits for your columns can be tricky, especially when you are just getting started. You should start with your gut feeling, run a few sprints, and refine the limits as you and your team get a better feel for the workflow. One way to get started is to base your limits on the number of people you have on your team. For example, if you have five developers, then your maximum limit for your **In Progress** columns (assuming this means development) should be no more than five, as it is not logical to have five people working on six issues at the same time.

So, if we look at the example in the preceding screenshot, we are over the maximum limit for the **In Progress** column. This could mean that the team, especially the developers, has overcommitted on their tasks; someone might have decided to work on two tasks in parallel. This is causing a bottleneck, and issues are not being completed quickly enough to move to the **In Review** column, causing a minimum limit violation, where you have reviewers waiting around for work. This data can be very useful in your sprint retrospective meetings to help you review the problem and refine the process.

So, as you can see, setting column constraints is situational, and is based on your team's composition as well as their abilities. As things change, you will need to change your limits accordingly. Remember, the goal here is to measure, identify, and improve.

Kanplan

The second mixed agile methodology is called **Kanplan**. As the name suggests, this methodology leans more toward Kanban than Scrum. In a nutshell, Kanplan allows you to have a more robust backlog, while still allowing you time to enjoy the flexibility of Kanban.

As we have seen in the previous chapter, by default, a Kanban board does not have a true backlog. You will usually use the first column on the board as the backlog. While this approach works when you are just getting started, very soon it will become very hard to manage as the number of items in the column grows. This makes it difficult to get a good grasp on all the outstanding issues, and also causes trouble when your team tries to prioritize things to work on, especially if they have also defined custom swimlanes for your board.

To enable backlog for a Kanban board, follow these steps:

1. Navigate to the Kanban board that you want to add a backlog for.
2. Click on the **Board** drop-down menu and select the **Configure** option.
3. Select the **Columns** option from the left-hand panel.
4. Drag one or more workflow statuses into the **Kanban backlog** section on the left:

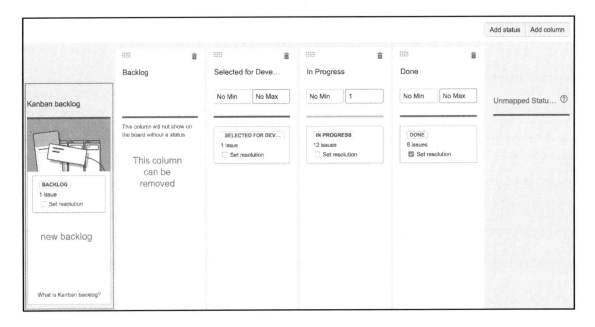

As shown in the preceding screenshot, we have a **Backlog** column in our Kanban columns setup, but since we now want to use the backlog feature, we move the **Backlog** status to the Kanban backlog column instead.

The new Kanban backlog works just like any board columns: You can have more than one status mapped to it, so any issues in one of the mapped statuses will appear in the new backlog. Note that because of this, any issues that are not in a mapped status will not appear in the new backlog, so make sure you add all the appropriate statuses.

 Simply mapping all your existing statuses in the default **Backlog** column to the new Kanban backlog would be the easiest way to ensure you do not leave any issues off.

Once you have enabled backlog for your Kanban board, you will see the new **Backlog** option at the top of the left-hand navigation panel when you go to your project. Clicking on that will show you a very similar interface to Scrum, as shown in the following screenshot:

Just like a Scrum' backlog, all issues are ordered from top to bottom. You can drag any issue up and down the backlog queue to prioritize it. For issues that are at the very bottom, you can right-click on the issue and send it straight to the top.

One key difference between a Kanban backlog and a Scrum backlog is that since Kanban does not have sprints, you do not create them and then add issues to the sprints. Instead, you add issues to the next status or column in the workflow. In the example shown in the preceding screenshot, this is the **Selected for Development** column. If you are familiar with Scrum, that is the section where your new sprint is, and you will be adding issues into the sprint. Here in Kanban, you are prioritizing and moving issues from the backlog's **to-do list** into an **action list**. With this change, your new Kanban board will look something similar to the one shown in the following screenshot, where the board will focus on the actual issues that have been prioritized without the noise of a big overwhelming **Backlog** column to distract your team with:

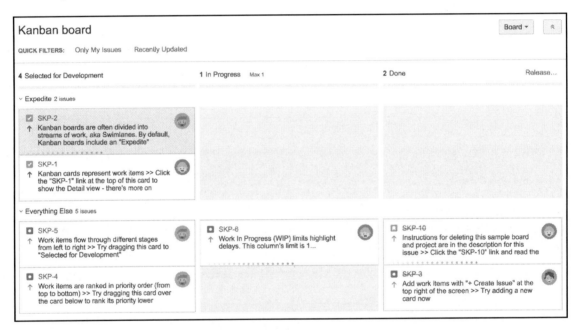

And this is not where the new Kanplan backlog stops. By leveraging the same backlog feature available to Scrum, you now also get access to features such as managing your issues with epics in a visual way, just like in Scrum. This is especially helpful for Scrum teams that are just starting to move toward using Kanplan. The epics panel for your backlog should be enabled by default, but if for some reason it is not, you can always manually enable it by going to the **Column management** page of your agile board's configuration panel:

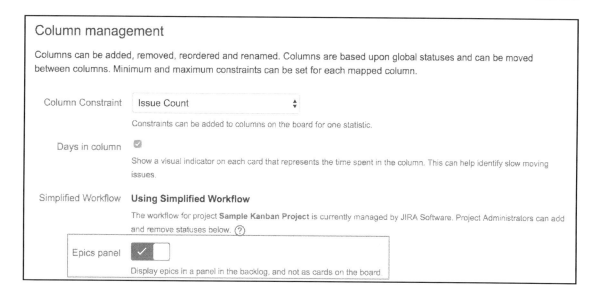

Summary

In this chapter, we looked at different ways to customize and manage your agile board in Jira. Some of the important points we have covered include managing the permissions and scopes of an agile board, customizing the board's columns, mapping board columns to Jira workflow statuses, and using swimlanes to group similar issues to better categorize our issues.

We also touched on some concepts in Jira, such as permissions and workflows. In the next chapter, we will take a deeper look into these core features of Jira, and how you can customize and manage them to suit your specific needs.

5
Customizing Jira Software

In the previous chapters, we created both Scrum and Kanban projects using Jira's agile project templates. With these templates, a default set of configurations is automatically created and applied to our projects, such as the types of issue we can create and fields that we need to fill in when creating new issues. As your projects become more complex and new requirements come up, you will quickly find you need to be able to have more control over your project settings.

By the end of the chapter, you will have learned how to:

- Create your own issue types and make them available to your projects
- Add new custom fields to collect more relevant data from users
- Customize workflows to better mimic your processes
- Secure your Jira with different levels of permission control
- Manage email notifications sent out from Jira to notify users of changes to issues

Customizing issue types

Each issue has a type (therefore, the name "issue type"), which is represented by the issue type field. This lets you know what type of issue it is; for example, if the issue is a bug or a feature. Jira comes with a list of pre-defined issue types, such as Story, Epic, and Task.

The default issue types are great for simple software development projects, but they do not necessarily meet the needs of others. Since it is impossible to create a system that can address everyone's needs, Jira lets you create your own issue types and assigns them to projects. For example, for a help desk project, you might want to create a custom issue type called **ticket**. You can create this custom issue type and assign it to the **Help Desk** project and users will be able to log tickets, instead of bugs, in the system as shown here:

1. Log in to Jira as a Jira administrator.
2. Browse to the Jira administration console.
3. Select the **Issues** tab and then the **Issue types** option:

Issue types			Add issue type ⑦
Name	**Type**	**Related Schemes**	**Actions**
▣ **Bug** A problem which impairs or prevents the functions of the product.	Standard	• SSP: Scrum Issue Type Scheme • KANBAN: Kanban Issue Type Scheme	Edit Delete Translate
▣ **Epic** Created by JIRA Software - do not edit or delete. Issue type for a big user story that needs to be broken down.	Standard	• Default Issue Type Scheme • SSP: Scrum Issue Type Scheme • KANBAN: Kanban Issue Type Scheme	Edit Delete Translate
▢ **Story** Created by JIRA Software - do not edit or delete. Issue type for a user story.	Standard	• Default Issue Type Scheme • SSP: Scrum Issue Type Scheme • KANBAN: Kanban Issue Type Scheme	Edit Delete Translate
☑ **Task** A task that needs to be done.	Standard	• SSP: Scrum Issue Type Scheme • KANBAN: Kanban Issue Type Scheme	Edit Delete Translate
▢ **Sub-task** The sub-task of the issue	Sub-Task	• SSP: Scrum Issue Type Scheme • KANBAN: Kanban Issue Type Scheme	Edit Delete Translate

4. Click on the **Add issue type** button.
5. Enter the name and description for the new issue type.

6. Select whether the new issue type will be a **Standard Issue Type** or a **Sub-Task Issue Type**:

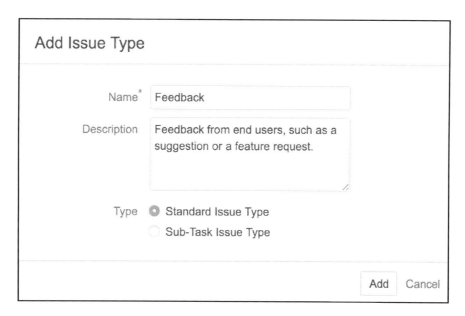

7. Click on **Add** to create the new issue type.

After you have created your new issue type, you will need to make it available to the project. You can do this by adding the new issue type to the *issue type scheme* used by the project. An issue type scheme contains a list of issue types, and is applied to one or more projects. This way, a project can have its own set of issue types, or have a shared set of issue types with other similar projects. To add your new issue type to an issue type scheme:

1. Browse to the Jira administration console.
2. Select the **Issues** tab and then the **Issue types schemes** option.
3. Look for the issue type scheme used by the project and click its **Edit** link.
4. Drag and drop the new issue type from the right **Available Issue Types** column to the left **Issue Types for Current Scheme** column.

5. Click the **Save** button:

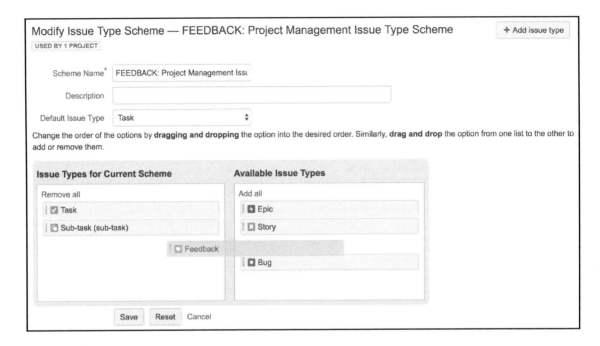

Adding new custom fields

Just like issue types, Jira comes with a number of built-in fields. You have already seen a few of them in the previous chapters. For example, when creating new stories for your agile boards, there are fields such as summary, priority, and assignee. These fields make up the backbone of an issue, and you cannot remove them from the system. For this reason, they are referred to as **system fields**.

While Jira's built-in fields are quite comprehensive for agile software development uses, most organizations soon find they have special requirements that cannot be addressed simply with the default fields available. To help you tailor Jira to your organization's needs, Jira lets you create and add your own fields to the system, called **custom fields**.

Jira comes with many types of custom fields, ranging from simple text fields, and select lists, to more complex ones, such as cascading select lists and user selectors. And if you find these are not sufficient enough, there are many more you can get from the Atlassian Marketplace, where you can find more specialized fields that talk to Salesforce.com, and many more. To start adding new custom fields to Jira:

1. Browse to the Jira administration console.
2. Select the **Issues** tab and then the **Custom fields** option.
3. Click on the **Add Custom Field** button. This will bring you to step 1 of the process, where you can select the custom field type.
4. Search and select the custom field type you wish to add, and click on **Next**. This will bring you to step 2 of the process, where you can specify the custom field's name and options:

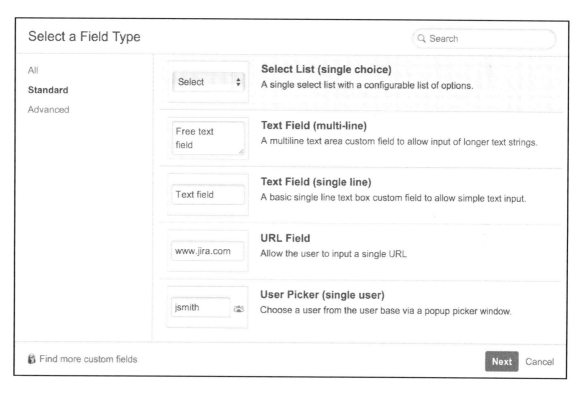

If you do not see the field type you are looking for, select the **All** option from the left-hand side and then search again.

5. Enter values for the **Name** and **Description** fields. If you are creating a selection-based custom field, such as a select list, you will need to add its select options too (you can update this list later):

6. Click on the **Create** button. This will bring you to the last step of the process, where you can specify the screen to which you would like to add the field.
7. Select the screens and click on **Update**. The following screenshot shows that the newly created field has been added to both of the support screens:

Associate field Origin to screens

Associate the field Origin to the appropriate screens. You must associate a field to a screen before it will be displayed.
New fields will be added to the end of a tab.

Screen	Tab	Select
Default Screen	Field Tab	☐
Resolve Issue Screen	Field Tab	☐
SKP: Kanban Bug Screen	Field Tab	☐
SKP: Kanban Default Issue Screen	Field Tab	☐
SSP: Scrum Bug Screen	Field Tab	☐
SSP: Scrum Default Issue Screen	Field Tab	☐
SUPPORT: Task Management Create Issue Screen	Field Tab	☑
SUPPORT: Task Management Edit/View Issue Screen	Field Tab	☑
Workflow Screen	Field Tab	☐

[Update] Cancel

After you have created the custom field, you can always come back later and customize it. For example, with our origin select list field, we have added three options when creating the field. If more options are needed, we can edit the field and add more options to it.

Customizing Jira workflows

Up until now, all the Scrum and Kanban projects we have created have their own workflow, named `Software Simplified Workflow` for Project X, and this is what is called the **Simplified Workflow**. A simplified workflow is a type of workflow that is designed specifically to work with agile projects, by having minimum restrictions. This means:

- There is a pre-defined set of statuses/columns for both Scrum and Kanban
- Board administrators can easily make changes, by simply adding and removing columns

- Issues can be moved between the statuses/columns freely with no restrictions
- There are no intermediate screens when an issue is being moved

This is great for most standard agile projects, where the goal is to have a straightforward workflow, and freedom for team members to move issues on the board as needed. However, sometimes you will have special requirements around your processes and your workflow will need to reflect those. For example, you might have a validation requirement that an issue can only be closed if a quality assurance engineer has signed off on it, or you might have a security requirement that only members of a certain group can move an issue to a target status.

These requirements may seem counter-intuitive in an agile environment, but remember that nothing is a one size fits all solution, and Jira lets you customize the workflow used by your project to best fulfill all your needs.

Jira comes with a very intuitive graphical tool to help you, as a Jira administrator, to create and customize your workflows. The following is a screenshot of how Jira visually represents a workflow in the tool:

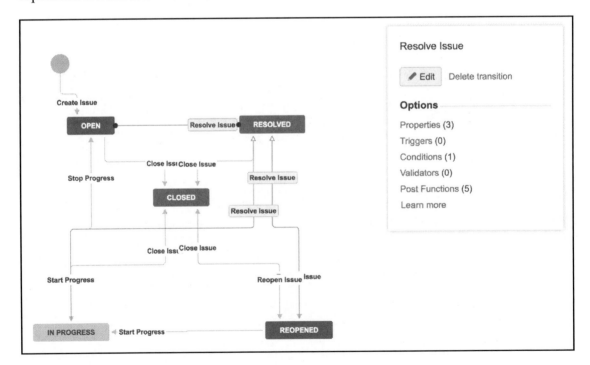

Each **status** is represented as a box. Each **transition** is represented as a line between two statuses. When clicking on either a status or a transition, a properties panel will appear on the right-hand side, allowing you to further customize it.

Authoring a workflow

So, let's take a look at how to create and set up a new workflow in Jira. To create a new workflow, all you need is a name and description:

1. Browse to the Jira administration console.
2. Select the **Issues** tab and then the **Workflows** option.
3. Click on the **Add Workflow** button.
4. Enter a name and description for the new workflow in the **Add Workflow** dialog.
5. Click on the **Add** button to create the workflow.

The newly created workflow will only contain the default create and open status, so you will need to configure it by adding new statuses and transitions to make it useful. Let's start with adding new statuses to the workflow using the following steps:

1. Click on the **Add status** button.
2. Select an existing status from the drop-down list. If the status you need does not exist, you can create a new status by entering its name and pressing the *Enter* key on your keyboard.
3. Check the **Allow all statuses to transition to this one** option, if you want users to be able to move the issue into this status regardless of its current status. This will create a **Global Transition**, which is a convenient way to allow an issue to use this transition from any status to get to the target status.

4. Click on the **Add** button to add the status to your workflow. You can repeat these steps to add as many statuses as you want to your workflow:

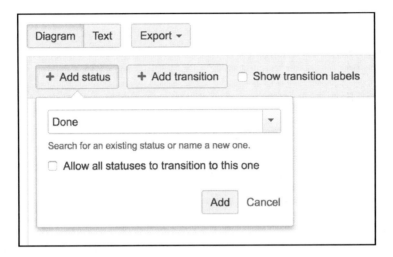

Try to re-use existing statuses if possible, so you do not end up with many similar statuses to manage.

Now that the statuses are added to the workflow, they need to be linked with transitions, so issues can move from one status to the next. There are two ways to create a transition:

- Click on the **Add transition** button or you can follow the next step
- Select the originating status, then click and drag the arrow to the destination status

Both options will bring up the **Add transition** dialog, as shown in the following screenshot:

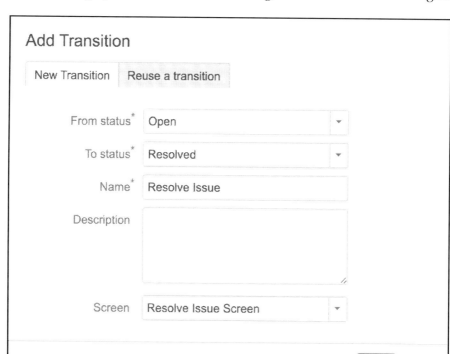

From the preceding screenshot, you can choose to either create a new transition with the **New Transition** tab or use an existing transition with the **Reuse a transition** tab.

When creating a new transition, you will need to configure the following:

- **From status**: The originating status. The transition will be available when the issue is in the selected status.
- **To status**: The destination status. Once the transition is executed, the issue will be put into the selected status.
- **Name**: Name of the transition. This is the text that will be displayed to users. It is usually a good idea to name your transitions starting with a verb, such as `Close Issue` or `Submit for Review`.
- **Description**: An optional text description is the purpose of this transition. This will not be displayed to users.

- **Screen**: An optional intermediate screen to be displayed when users execute the transition. For example, you display a screen to capture additional data as part of the transition. If you do not select a screen, the transition will be executed immediately. The following screenshot shows a workflow screen:

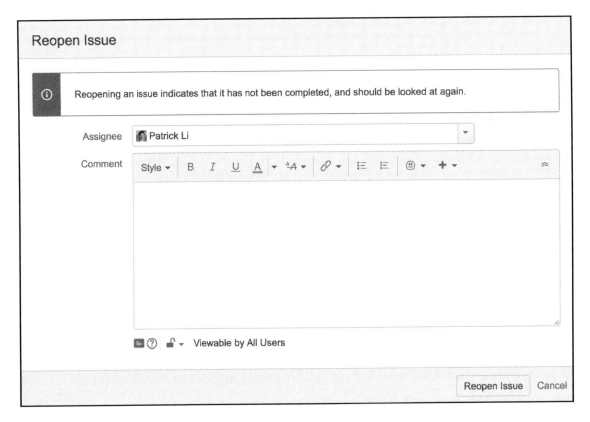

If you want to reuse an existing transition, simply select the **Reuse a transition** tab, the **From status** and **To status**, and the transition to reuse, as shown in the following screenshot:

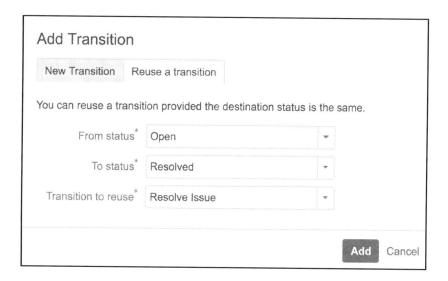

 Jira will only list valid transitions based on the **To status** selection.

You might be wondering when you should create a new transition and when you should reuse an existing transition. The big difference between the two is that when you reuse a transition, all instances of the reused transition, also known as **common transition**, will share the same set of configurations, such as conditions and validators. Also, any changes made to the transition will be applied to all instances. A good use case for this is when you need to have multiple transitions with the same name and setup, such as **Close Issue**; instead of creating separate transitions each time, you can create one transition and reuse it whenever you need a transition to close an issue. Later on, if you need to add a new validator to the transition to validate additional user input, you will only need to make the change once, rather than multiple times for each **Close Issue** transition.

Another good practice to keep in mind is to not have a *dead end* state in your workflow, for example, allowing closed issues to be reopened. This will prevent users from accidentally closing an issue and not being able to correct the mistake.

Now that we have seen how to add new statuses and transitions to a workflow, let's look at adding conditions, validators, and post functions to a transition.

Adding a condition to transitions

New transitions do not have any conditions by default. This means that anyone who has access to the issue will be able to execute the transition. By adding a condition to a workflow transition, you can control who or when an issue can be transitioned.

 Conditions take place before a transition is executed.

Jira allows you to add any number of conditions to the transition:

1. Select the transition you want to add conditions to.
2. Click on the **Conditions** link.
3. Click on the **Add condition** link. This will bring you to the **Add Condition To transition** page, which lists all the available conditions you can add.
4. Select the condition you want to add.
5. Click on the **Add** button to add the condition.
6. Depending on the condition, you may be presented with the **Add Parameters To Condition** page, where you can specify the configuration options for the condition. For example, the **User Is In Group** condition will ask you to select the group to check against.

Newly added conditions are appended to the end of the existing list of conditions, creating a **condition group**. By default, when there is more than one condition, a logical AND is used to group the conditions. This means that all conditions must pass for the entire condition group to pass. If one condition fails, the entire group fails, and the user will not be able to execute the transition. You can switch to use a logical OR, which means only one of the conditions in the group needs to pass for the entire group to pass. This is a very useful feature as it allows you to combine multiple conditions to form a more complex logical unit.

For example, the **User Is In Group** condition lets you specify a single group, but with the AND operator, you can add multiple **User Is In Group** conditions to ensure the user must exist in all the specific groups to be able to execute the transition. If you use the OR operator, then the user will only need to belong to one of the listed groups. The only restriction to this is that you cannot use both operators for the same condition group.

One transition can only have one condition group, and each condition group can only have one logical operator.

Adding a validator to transitions

Like conditions, transitions, by default, do not have any validators associated. This means transitions are completed as soon as they are executed. You can add validators to transitions to make sure that executions are only allowed to be completed when certain criteria are met. One good use case of validators is when a transition has a workflow screen to capture user input, and you need to validate the inputs, such as date format.

 Validators take place during a transition execution.

Perform the following steps to add a validator to a transition:

1. Select the transition you want to add validators to.
2. Click on the **Validators** link.
3. Click on the **Add validator** link. This will bring you to the **Add Validator To Transition** page, which lists all the available validators you can add.
4. Select the validator you want to add.
5. Click on the **Add** button to add the validator.
6. Depending on the validator, you may be presented with the **Add Parameters To Validator** page where you can specify configuration options for the validator. For example, the **Permissions** validator will ask you to select the permission to validate against.

Similar to conditions, when there are multiple validators added to a transition, they form a **validator group**. Unlike conditions, you can only use a logical AND for the group. This means that in order to complete a transition, every validator added to the transition must pass its validation criteria. Transitions cannot selectively pass validations using a logical OR.

The following screenshot shows a validator being placed on the transition, validating if the user has entered a value for the **Resolution Details** field:

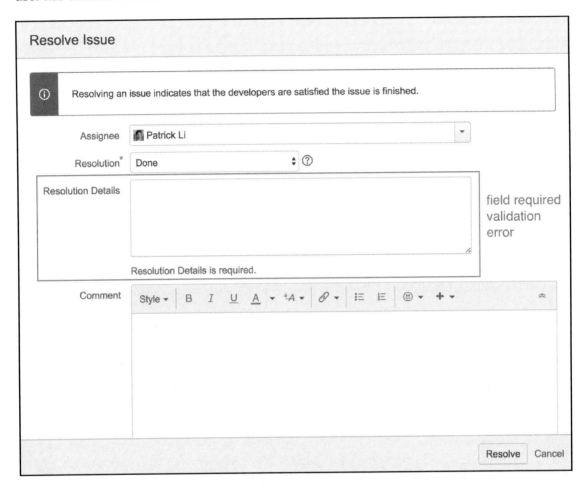

Adding a post function to transitions

Transitions, by default, are created with several post functions. These post functions provide key services to Jira's internal operations, so they cannot be deleted from the transition. These post functions perform the following:

- Set the issue status to the linked status of the destination workflow step
- Add a comment to an issue if one is entered during a transition

- Update the change history for an issue and store the issue in the database
- Re-index an issue to keep indexes in sync with the database
- Fire an event that can be processed by the listeners

As you can see, these post functions provide some of the basic functions such as updating a search index and setting an issue's status after transition execution, which are essential in Jira. Therefore, instead of users having to manually add them in and risk the possibility of leaving one or more out, Jira adds them for you automatically when you create a new transition.

 Post functions take place after a transition has successfully executed.

Perform the following steps to add a post function to a transition:

1. Select the transition you want to add post functions to.
2. Click on the **Post Functions** link.
3. Click on the **Add post function** link and select the post function you want to add.
4. Click on the **Add** button to add the post function.
5. Depending on the post function, you may be presented with the **Add Parameters To Function** page, where you can specify configuration options for the post function. The following screenshot shows an example from the **Update Issue Field** post function:

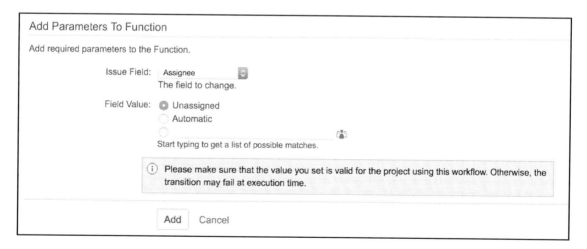

Just like conditions and validators, multiple post functions form a post function group in a transition. After a transition is executed, each post function in the group is executed sequentially as it appears in the list, from top to bottom. If any post function in the group encounters an error during processing, you will receive an error, and the remaining post functions will not be executed.

Since post functions are executed sequentially and some of them possess the abilities to modify values and perform other tasks, often, their sequence of execution becomes very important. For example, if you have a post function that changes the issue's assignee to the current user and another post function that updates an issue field's value with the issue's assignee, obviously the update assignee post function needs to occur first, so you need to make sure it is above the other post function.

You can move the positions of post functions up and down along the list by clicking on the **Move Up** and **Move Down** links. Note that not all post functions can be repositioned.

Managing Jira permissions

Security is the top most important priority in today's digital world. Ensuring only authorized personnel will have access to the data stored in Jira to prevent any potential information leak is something every Jira administrator needs to keep track of. To ensure there are proper security controls in place, Jira provides a number of options to control access permissions to the data it stores.

Global permissions

Global permissions, as the name suggests, is the highest permission level in Jira. These are coarse-grained permissions applied globally across Jira, controlling broad security levels, such as the ability to administer various configuration settings.

Global permissions can only be granted to groups. For this reason, you will need to organize your users into logical groups for global permissions to take effect. For example, you will want to have all your administrators belong to a single group, such as the `JIRA-administrators` group, so you can grant them administration permission:

1. Browse to the Jira administration console.
2. Select the **System** tab and then the **Global permissions** option.
3. Select the permission you wish to assign from the **Add Permission** section.
4. Choose the group to be given the permission.
5. Click on the **Add** button to add the assignment:

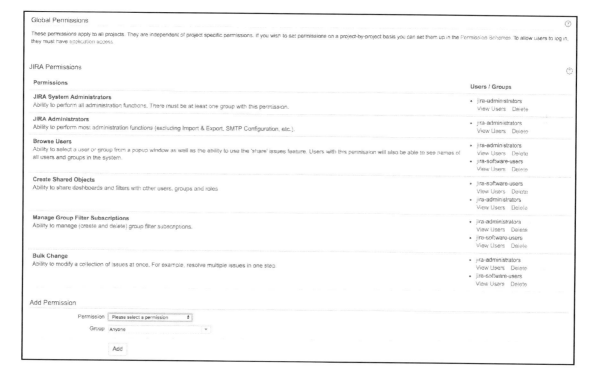

 A user with Jira Administrators' global permission cannot grant himself/herself Jira System Administrators' global permission.

Project permissions

As you have seen, global permissions controls mostly administration-level accesses, and in most cases, you will need the ability to control access to projects, such as who will be able to view and create new issues. This is where **permission schemes** come in.

A permission scheme defines a list of permissions available in Jira, such as who can delete an issue, and who can add comments, and lets you grant each permission to different users. This mapping of permission types to user definitions make up the permission scheme. Once you have defined the mapping for your scheme, you can then apply it to one or more projects. This gives you the flexibility to define unique permission settings for each project, as well as share and apply the same permission settings to multiple projects. To start working with permission schemes, perform the following steps:

1. Browse to the Jira administration console.
2. Select the **Issues** tab and then the **Permission schemes** option. By default, there should be two permission schemes already defined:
    - **Default permission scheme:** Default scheme used by non-agile projects.
    - **Default software scheme:** Default scheme used by all agile (Scrum and Kanban) projects.
      You can update the permission settings for the existing schemes by clicking on the **Permissions** link, which will affect all existing projects using the scheme, or create a new scheme by clicking the **Add permission scheme** button.
3. Once you have either selected or created the permission scheme you wish to configure, you will be taken to the **Edit Permissions** page, as shown in the following screenshot:

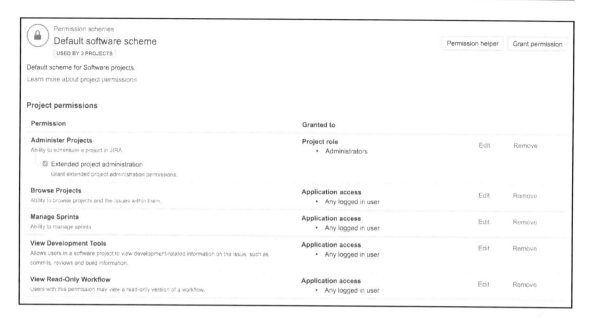

On this page, you will be presented with a list of project level permissions, along with short descriptions for each, and the users, groups, and roles that are linked to each of the permissions. You will notice that for the default permission scheme, most of the permission options have default users linked to them through project roles. If you are looking at a new permission scheme, there will be no users linked to any of the permissions. This is your one-page view of permission settings for projects, and you will also be able to add and delete users. To grant a permission to users:

1. Click on the **Grant permission** button or the **Edit** link for a specific permission.
2. Select the permissions you wish to grant the user.
3. Select the user option to specify whom to grant the permission to. Click on the **Show more** link to see more options.
4. Click on the **Grant** button to grant the selected permission.

5. Repeat this process to grant more users to the permission:

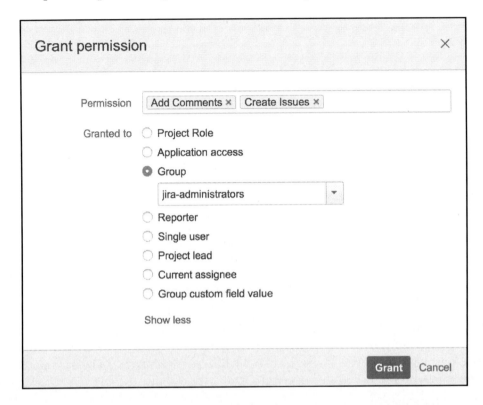

A permission option such as **User Custom Field Value** is a very flexible way to allow end users to control access. For example, you can have a custom field called **Editors**, and set up your **Edit Issues** permission to allow only users specified in the custom field to be able to edit issues. The custom field does not have to be placed on the usual view/edit screens for the permission to be applied. For example, you can have the custom field appear on a workflow transition called **Submit to Manager**; once the user has selected the manager, only the manager will have permission to edit the issue.

Issue permissions

A project level permission with a permission scheme is usually all you will need with your security requirements. However, sometimes you might need to take things one step further and control access permission on a per issue basis. One example of such a use case is when you have both internal and external users, such as customers working on the same project, and there are issues you do not want to share with your outside customers. In these cases, you can use **issue security schemes**.

Issue security allows users to set view permissions (not edit) on issues by selecting one of the preconfigured issue security levels from the system Security Level field. On a high level, issue security works in a similar way to permission schemes. The Jira administrator will start by creating and configuring a set of issue security schemes with security levels set. Project administrators can then apply one of these schemes to their projects, which allows the users (with **Set Issue Security** project permission) to select the security levels within the scheme and apply them to individual issues.

The starting point of using issue security is the issue security scheme. It is the responsibility of the Jira administrator to create and design the security levels so they can be reused as much as possible:

1. Browse to the Jira administration console.
2. Select the **Issues** tab and then the **Issue security schemes** option. Unlike permission schemes, there are no default issue security schemes available.
3. Click on the **Add Issue Security Scheme** button.
4. Enter a name and description for the new scheme.
5. Click on the **Add** button to create the new issue security scheme.
6. Click on the **Security Levels** link for the issue security scheme we just created. New issue security schemes do not contain any security levels, so we will need to add them manually.
7. Enter a name and description for the new security level in the **Add Security Level** section and click on the **Add Security Level** button. Repeat this step to add more security levels. With the security levels in place, we can now assign users who will have a view permission for each of the security levels.
8. Click on the **Add** link for the security level you wish to assign users to.
9. Select the option you wish to assign to the security level.
10. Click on the **Add** button to assign the users.

As shown in the following screenshot, we have two security levels defined, **Internal Only** and **Public**. So when an issue is set to have the Internal Only security level, only members of the demo-project-members group will be able to view the issue; anyone else will get a security error. When an issue is set to the Public security level, then anyone in Jira will be able to view the issue, provided they also meet the project level permissions set in the permission scheme used by the project:

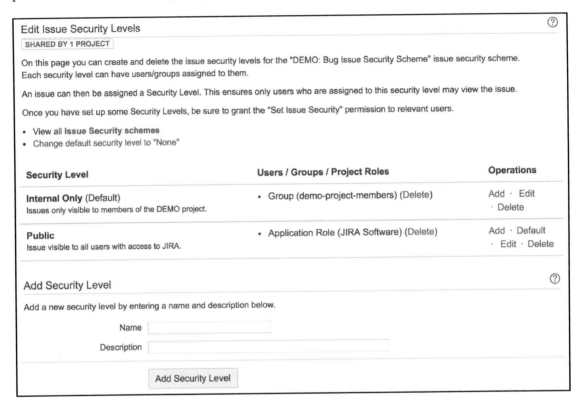

Troubleshooting permissions

Getting permission settings right is very critical to secure data for your organization, especially for projects containing sensitive information that require very restricted permission control. And with the different levels of permission controls in Jira, it can be frustrating and confusing to figure out why a user cannot access an issue he or she is expected to have access to.

To help with this, Jira provides a permission helper to assist administrators with pinpointing settings that prevent users from accessing certain features. To use the permission helper:

1. Browse to the Jira administration console.
2. Select the **System** tab and then the **Permission helper** option at the bottom.
3. Specify the user that is having access problems in the **User** field.
4. Specify the issue to test with.
5. Select the permission the user does not have (for example, **Edit Issues**).
6. Click on **Submit**:

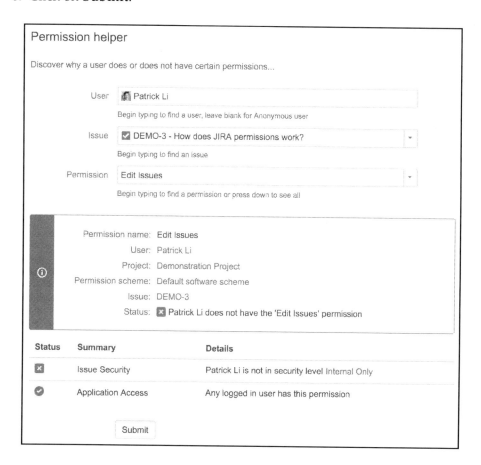

As shown in the preceding screenshot, the user **Patrick Li** cannot edit issue **DEMO-3** because he is not in the **Internal Only** issue security level, which is required as per the **Default Permission Scheme** used.

Managing Jira notifications

As your team starts to use Jira to run their projects day to day, each member would need to be notified when changes happen to the tasks they are working on, such as a quality assurance officer rejecting a bug fix submitted by an engineer, or a comment logged by the product owner on a new feature. This is especially important for distributed teams in different time zones, where simply walking up to someone for a quick chat is not an option. To help with collaboration within the team, Jira uses email notifications to keep everyone up to date on changes that happen to issues in the project, and it has a very flexible way to allow you to define how and when these notifications should be sent out.

Enabling outgoing emails

In order for Jira to send out outgoing email notifications, you need to be a Jira system administrator (for example, the user created during the initial setup is a system administrator) to configure mail server details. Perform the following steps to manage the outgoing mail server:

1. Browse to the Jira administration console.
2. Select the **System** tab and then the **Outgoing Mail** option. This will bring up the **Outgoing Mail** page:

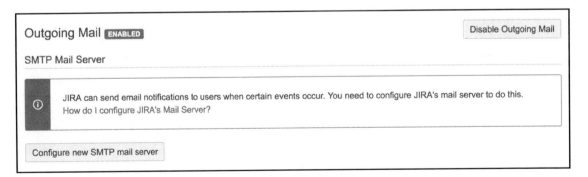

3. Click on the **Configure new SMTP mail server** button.

4. Enter the general details of your mail server, including the name, description, from address, and email prefix.
5. Select the type of mail server from the **Service Provider** field.
6. Enter the mail server's connection details.
7. Click on the **Test Connection** button to verify configuration.
8. Click on the **Add** button to register to the mail server:

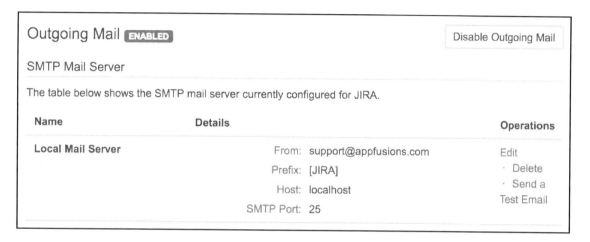

Once you have set up the SMTP mail server for your Jira instance, you will be able to send test emails to verify connectivity, which will be very useful during troubleshooting situations, as we will see later in this chapter. You can also disable all outgoing email notifications with the **Disable Outgoing Mail** button, a useful option if you want to temporarily disable all email notifications while you perform other maintenance tasks.

Configuring notification schemes

With the SMTP mail server setup, the next step is to configure rules for the following questions:

- When should Jira send out email notifications?
- Who should receive these email notifications?

Jira uses **notification schemes** to control the preceding two questions. In Jira, each user action, such as editing an issue, can trigger an event, and for each event, you can define a list of users that will receive notifications. This event to notification mapping is what makes up a notification scheme. Once you have defined your notification scheme, you can then apply the scheme to various projects. This way, each project can have its own unique notification settings, and multiple projects can share the same notification settings. To configure a notification scheme, perform the following steps:

1. Browse to the Jira administration console.

2. Select the **Issues** tab and then the **Notification schemes** option. This will bring up the **Notification Schemes** page. By default, there is only one notification scheme, called Default Notification Scheme, and all projects make use of it. You can choose to edit the default scheme by clicking on its **Notifications** link, which will affect all projects, or create a new scheme by clicking the **Add notification scheme** button.

3. Once you have the notification scheme ready, Jira will display the list of events available, and users (if any) that will receive notifications, as shown in the following screenshot:

Edit Notifications — Default Notification Scheme   ⑦

USED BY 7 PROJECTS

On this page you can edit the notifications for the "Default Notification Scheme" notification scheme.
- **Add notification**
- **View all** notification schemes

Event	Notifications	Actions
Issue Created (System)	• Current Assignee (Delete) • Reporter (Delete) • All Watchers (Delete)	Add
Issue Updated (System)	• Current Assignee (Delete) • Reporter (Delete) • All Watchers (Delete)	Add
Issue Assigned (System)	• Current Assignee (Delete) • Reporter (Delete) • All Watchers (Delete)	Add
Issue Resolved (System)	• Current Assignee (Delete) • Reporter (Delete) • All Watchers (Delete)	Add
Issue Closed (System)	• Current Assignee (Delete) • Reporter (Delete) • All Watchers (Delete)	Add

4. You can add new users to receive notifications by clicking the **Add** link for an event you want. Jira will then show you a list of all the options you can use to define the notification recipients. As you can see in the following screenshot, there are many options, ranging from static options, such as specific users in Jira or exact email addresses, to more dynamic options, such as all users in a group or in a custom field of the issue.

5. Select the notification recipient option and click **Add**. You can repeat the process to add more users to receive notifications for the event:

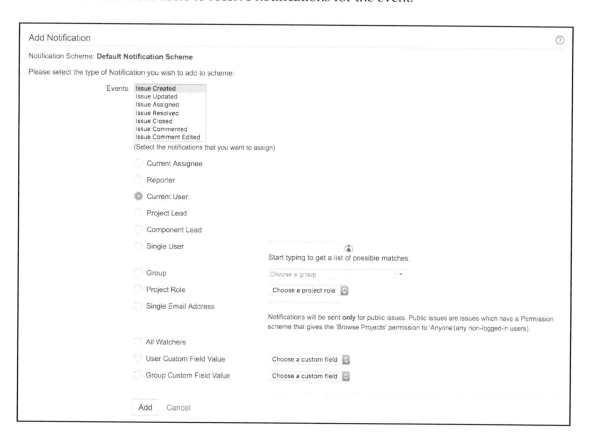

Troubleshooting notifications

Often, as an administrator, when people do not receive expected notifications from Jira, it can be difficult and frustrating to find the cause. There are two common causes for notification-related problems: outgoing mail server connectivity, or misconfiguration of the notification scheme.

Troubleshooting outgoing mail server problems is quite simple. All you need to do is try to send out a test email from the **Send a Test Email** option from the **Outgoing Mail** administration section. If you receive your test email, then there will be no problems with your outgoing mail server configuration, and you can focus on your notification configurations. As shown in the following screenshot, the test email delivery has failed, and the error is because Jira was unable to connect to the configured SMTP server:

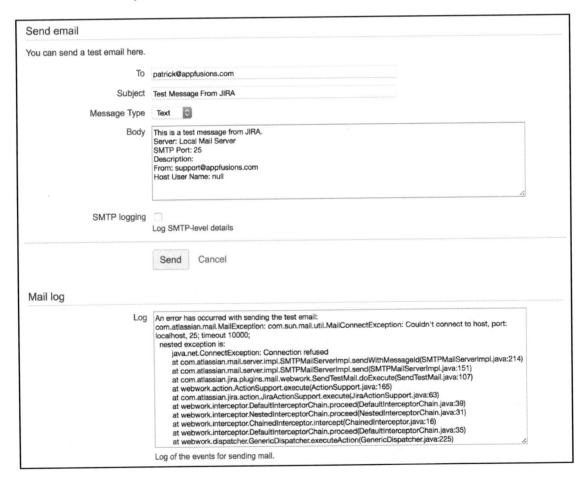

Troubleshooting notification settings is not as straightforward, since there are a number of things that you will need to consider. To help with this challenge, Jira has a new feature, called **Notification helper**. The notification helper can save the Jira administrators time by helping them to pinpoint why a given user does or does not receive notifications. All the administrator has to do is tell the helper who the user is, which issue (or an example issue from the target project) the user should be receiving notifications for, and the event that is triggering the notification:

1. Browse to the Jira administration console.
2. Select the **System** tab and then the **Notification helper** option.
3. Specify the user that should receive notifications in the **User** field.
4. Specify the issue to test with.
5. Select the type of notification event.
6. Click on **Submit**.

Notification helper will then process the input and report if the user is expected to receiving be notifications and why, based on notification scheme settings:

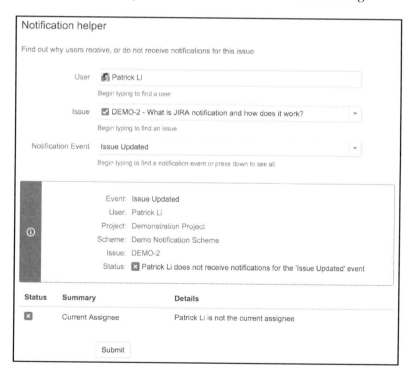

As you can see from the preceding screenshot, the user **Patrick Li** is currently not receiving notifications for the **DEMO-2** issue when it is updated because the notification is set up to have only the **Current Assignee** receive emails, and **Patrick Li** is not the assignee.

Summary

In this chapter, we looked at how to customize Jira beyond the default templates provided by its agile templates. We looked at how to create new issue types and custom fields, as well as authoring workflows with custom permission and validations. We also introduced Jira's permission hierarchy and the options you have to secure your system against unauthorized access. Lastly, we looked at how to manage email notifications in Jira, so team members can stay up to date on changes that happen in their projects.

In the next chapter, we will look at some advanced topics, such as integrating Jira with other tools to go beyond what it can do with out-of-the box features.

6
Jira Software – Advanced

In the previous chapters, we looked at how to use Jira to run and manage projects with both Scrum and Kanban, as well as customizing Jira itself to be more flexible and adaptable to your needs. In this chapter, we will look into some of the additional capabilities of Jira, as well as integrating with other systems to provide a complete end-to-end experience for you and your team.

By the end of the chapter, you will have learned how to:

- Display and share project information with the dashboard
- Create and link epics to requirement pages
- Create user stories from requirement pages
- Display sprints on calendars
- Capture sprint meeting notes
- Share reports on project progress
- Print out your agile cards and pin them onto a physical board

Displaying agile reports

As we saw in Chapter 2, *Jira Software for Scrum* and Chapter 3, *Jira Software for Kanban*, Jira comes with a number of reports that you can generate to get a better understanding of how your project is tracking. However, they often require you to go to your board and then generate the report manually. A better way to display and share information on your project is to take advantage of some of Jira's built-in collaboration features.

Using the Jira dashboard

The easiest way to display and share your project and sprint progress with everyone is to use the dashboard feature from Jira. A dashboard acts as a portal page for your project, and you can display different information about your project by adding gadgets onto the dashboard.

Jira comes with a number of gadgets that are designed specifically to display agile related information, including:

- **Sprint burndown gadget**: This displays a burndown chart of your sprint on the dashboard. The chart will be automatically updated to reflect the current data.
- **Days remaining in sprint gadget**: This displays how many days are left before the sprint is scheduled to be completed. It acts as a reminder for how much time is left on the clock.
- **Sprint health gadget**: This displays a bar chart showing information on how the sprint is progressing; for example, how much more work is still left to do.

The power of using the Jira dashboard is that you are not limited to using only the gadgets that are specifically designed for Agile. Jira comes with many other useful gadgets that you can use to drill down into your project and sprint. They are as follows:

- **Filter results gadget**: You can select a filter and display the result in a table. You can use this to display the most important issues in the sprint.
- **Two-dimensional filter statistics gadget**: This is similar to the filter results gadget, but instead of displaying a list of issues, it will display a statistical breakdown of the filter result based on the fields you choose.
- **Pie chart gadget**: You can select a filter and the result will be displayed as a pie chart, where each slice is based on a field of your choice; for example, priority.

As you can see, you can build a very useful dashboard by combining gadgets from both agile and non-agile based ones. You can even create your own gadget or download gadgets from third-party vendors to display information specific to your needs.

To create a dashboard for your project and sprint, perform the following steps:

1. Select the **Manage Dashboards** option from the **Dashboards** menu.
2. Click on the **Create new dashboard** button.
3. Enter a name for your new dashboard.

4. Select how you want to share the dashboard. Dashboards are private by default, so for others to see the dashboard, you must share the dashboard with them. As shown in the following screenshot, we are sharing the dashboard with members of the **Top Secret Project**.

5. Click on the **Add** button to create the dashboard:

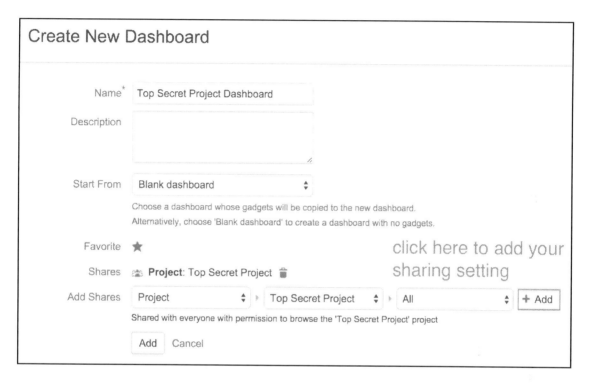

Make sure you click the **Add** button after you have selected who to share the dashboard with.

Once you have created a new dashboard, you can start adding contents onto it with gadgets:

1. Click on the **Add a new gadget** link. It does not matter which one you click, as you can always reposition the gadgets after they have been added, by simply dragging them around on the dashboard.

2. Select the gadgets you want to add from the **Add a gadget** dialog by clicking on its **Add gadget** button.

3. Close the dialog once you have added all the gadgets you want:

Once you have added the gadgets, you will need to configure each gadget to display the data you want. For most gadgets, all you need to do is select the board, sprint, project, or filter to use:

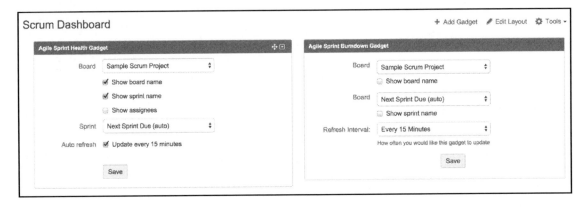

You can also configure the layout of the dashboard. By default, the dashboard is divided into two columns of equal width. You can change that by clicking on the **Edit Layout** button and then selecting the layout you want.

Using the wallboard

Another great Jira feature you can take advantage of is the wallboard. You can think of wallboards as Jira dashboards that you display on a big wall using a projector, or with a big monitor.

Using a wallboard is a great way to share information about your project with your team and other colleagues. The following screenshot shows an example of a wallboard. By taking the data out of an agile project, and projecting that onto a big screen, everyone will have instant and easy access to the information they need. As people walk by your team's work area, they will get a good idea of how the team is progressing:

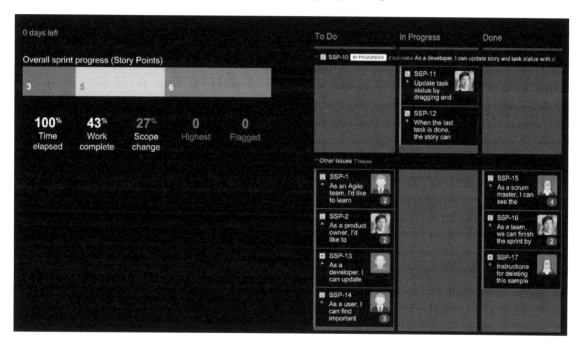

To set up a wallboard for your agile project, you will first need to create a dashboard. Note that not all gadgets are wallboard-compatible, but all the agile gadgets that come out of the box are compatible. Once you have your dashboard ready, click on the **Tools** menu and select the **View as Wallboard** option, link it up to a big monitor, and you have yourself an awesome wallboard.

If you have multiple dashboards, you can create a slideshow of wallboards. All you have to do is select the **Setup Wallboard Slideshow** option from the **Tools** menu, as shown in the following screenshot, to set up the slideshow. Select the dashboards to include on the wall, and how you would like the slideshow to look like(**Display Options**), and use the **View as Wallboard Slideshow** option to display it:

Integrating Jira with Confluence

Confluence is a team collaboration solution from Atlassian (the maker of Jira) that enables teams to collaborate and create content together. Organizations often use it to create and share information related to projects, such as functional and design specifications. Jira works seamlessly with Confluence to provide you with a complete agile experience. In the following sections, we will look at how you can integrate Jira with Confluence to:

- Create epics and user stories with design documentation
- Manage and view your sprints on a calendar
- Capture meeting notes for your sprint planning sessions

- Create retrospective reports at the end of each sprint
- Share and publish release information

Setting up an application link with Confluence

If you have not already integrated Jira and Confluence together, you need to create a new application link. To create an application link with Confluence, perform the following steps:

1. Browse to the Jira administration console.
2. Select the **Applications** tab and then the **Application links** option.
3. Enter the URL to your Confluence instance and click on the **Create new link** button, as shown in the next screenshot:

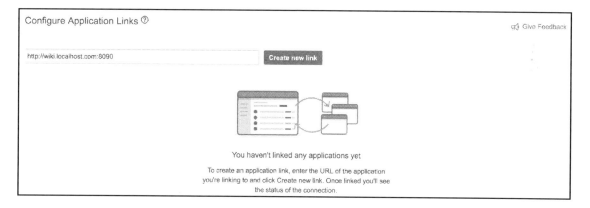

4. Tick the **The servers have the same set of users and usernames** option if both Jira and Confluence share the same user repository; for example, LDAP.

If you have a common user repository for both applications, such as LDAP, by enabling this option, users will have a seamless experience. Otherwise, they will be prompted to authorize access for the first-time viewing of contents from the other application.

5. Tick the **I am an administrator on both instances** option if you have an administrator account on both Jira and Confluence. This will let you also create a reciprocal link from Confluence to Jira.

6. Click on the **Continue** button:

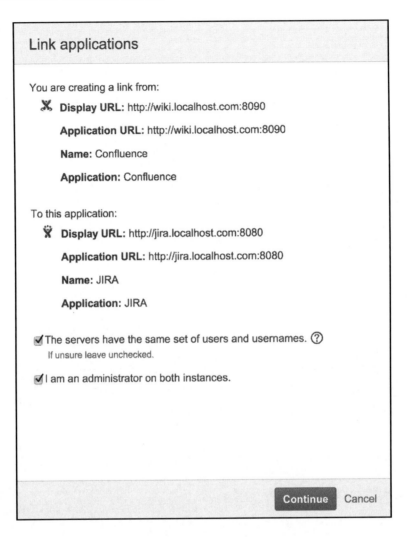

7. Verify that the onscreen information is correct. If both applications are able to communicate with each other successfully, it will display the URLs and application name and type, as shown in the following screenshot. Then, click on the **Continue** button:

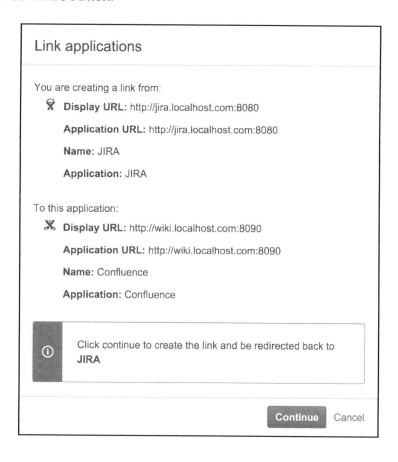

8. Continue with the onscreen wizard, and once the application link is successfully created, you will see a success message and the new application link listed for Confluence:

Creating Confluence pages from epics

Jira is a great tool to track and manage your day-to-day activities for your project, but it is not the best tool to capture detailed information for your tasks, such as design documentation and functional specifications for your epics. With Confluence as a documentation platform, there are a few ways you can create design documents and link them to your epics.

The first option is to create your documents called Confluence pages, directly from your agile board's backlog:

1. Browse to your agile board and go to its backlog.
2. Open up the **Epics** panel from the left-hand side.
3. Select and expand the epic you want to create a Confluence page for.
4. Click on the **Links pages** link from the epic.

5. Click on the **Create page** button from the dialog, as shown in the following screenshot:

6. After you click on the **Create page** button, you will be taken to Confluence in a new browser tab with the **Create** dialog displayed, as shown in the following screenshot. By default, the dialog will have the **Project requirements** template (also called a blueprint) preselected for you, but you can choose to use a different template if you want. Also note that the **Select space** field at the top will have the last Confluence space you have visited preselected, so make sure you select the correct space to create your new page in.

7. Click on the **Create** button after you have selected the correct space to create your new page in:

8. If this is the first time you have used the product requirements template, you will get a **Let's get started** information dialog, as seen in the following screenshot. Simply tick the **Don't show this again** option at the bottom and click on the **Create** button to create your new page:

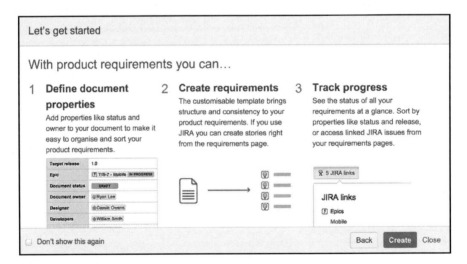

9. Click on the **Create** button again to start working on the new page.

Confluence will present you with a new page and editor, with a predefined template. You can simply fill in the templates with information such as goals and requirements. A few important things to note:

- Make sure you give your page a title. A good practice is to name it after the linked epic.
- Reference the epic in Jira by clicking on the **Link to related Jira epic of feature** text label from the **Epic** field. This way, a reference link will be created between the requirement page and the epic issue.

With the page created, if you go back to Jira, the **Linked pages** link for the epic will change to **1 linked page**, and clicking on that will show you the actual linked page, as shown in the following screenshot:

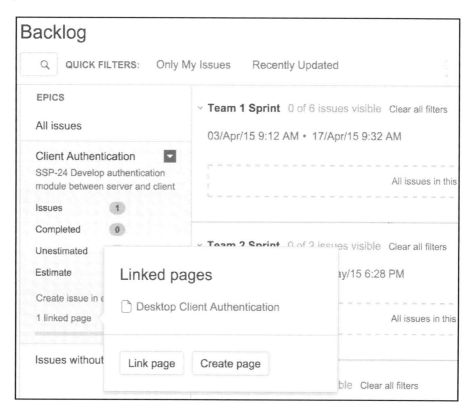

If you already have requirement pages created for the project, instead of creating new ones from the epics, you can simply link to those pages by clicking on the **Link page** button. After clicking on it, you will get a search box, and you can type in your page's title, find the page you want, and select it to create a link. This is illustrated in the next screenshot:

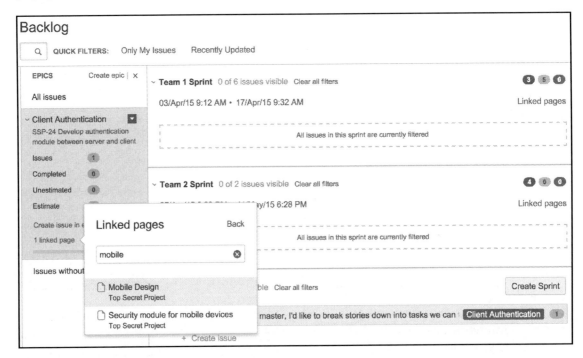

 If you cannot see the linked pages, make sure Confluence has the remote API enabled. See `https://confluence.atlassian.com/x/vEsC` for more details.

Creating user stories from Confluence

If you are using the product requirements blueprint, as we have seen earlier, there is a section on the page for you to list out all the requirements for the feature. Once you have defined all the requirements with the team, you can create user stories directly on the page. To do this, perform the following steps:

1. Go to your product requirements page in Confluence.
2. Highlight the text of the requirement you want to create a user story with. The text you highlight will become the summary of the user story, as shown in the following screenshot:

Requirements

#	💬 ✗	User Story	Importance	Notes
1	Responsive width to auto-adjust depending on screen size		Must Have	
2	Reduce on-screen assets to simplify UI		Must Have	
3			Nice to have	

3. Click the Jira icon. This will open up the **Create Issue** dialog, as shown in the following screenshot.
4. Make sure the project and issue type selection is correct. You can click on the **Edit** link to change that.
5. Enter a description for the user story.
6. If the **Product Requirements** page is already linked to an epic in Jira, you will see a **Link to epic** option. Uncheck this option if you do not want the user story to be added to the epic.

7. Click on the **Create** button to create the user story:

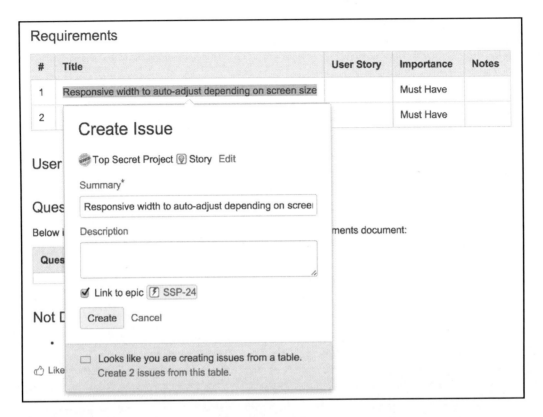

If you have multiple requirements listed in the **Requirements** table on your page, you can click on the **Create x issues from this table** option at the bottom, and Confluence will automatically create a user story for each requirement you have.

After you have created the user stories, you will see a Jira issue added next to each of the requirements, showing their key and status. Their status will be automatically updated as the issues are being worked on. You will also see a **Jira links** button at the top of the page next to the breadcrumbs. Clicking on that will display all the Jira issues currently linked to this page, including any epics and user stories. Refer to the following screenshot:

 Currently, the Jira links button is only available if you use the default theme in Confluence.

Planning your sprints with team calendars

As you and your team work on the sprint, it is often helpful to see how your sprints fit in with other activities your team might have: for example, if there are team members going on a vacation or with travel plans halfway through a sprint, or if there are other delivery commitments that might interfere with the sprint.

The key to solving this is to have all this information visually displayed on a single calendar, viewable and shared by the entire team, so everyone can stay well-informed, just like having tasks plotted on an agile board. To do this, perform the following steps:

1. Browse to your team's **Team Calendar**.
2. Click on the **Add Event** button.
3. Select the **Jira Agile Sprints** option for **Event Type**:

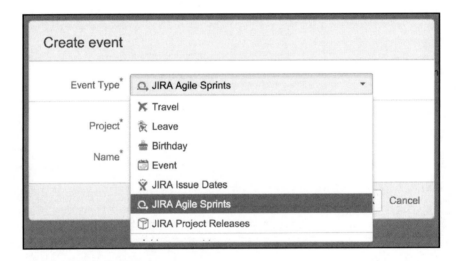

4. Select the project that belongs to your Scrum board.
5. Enter a name for the event.
6. Click on the **OK** button to create the event.

 Team Calendars for Confluence is a separate product you can get for Confluence from Atlassian Marketplace
at https://marketplace.atlassian.com/plugins/com.atlassian.conflu
ence.extra.team-calendars/cloud/overview

Once you have created the event, Team Calendar will get all the sprints you have for the selected project, and display them on the calendar. As shown in the following screenshot, we have two sprints, **Sprint 2** and **Sprint 3**. We can also see that **Tom Johnson** will be away at the start of **Sprint 2**, which might have an impact on the team's ability to complete everything in the sprint on time. Also, if you have all team members' vacation plans on the calendar, then during your sprint planning sessions, you will have all the information you need when deciding how much work should go into the sprint and how long the sprint should be:

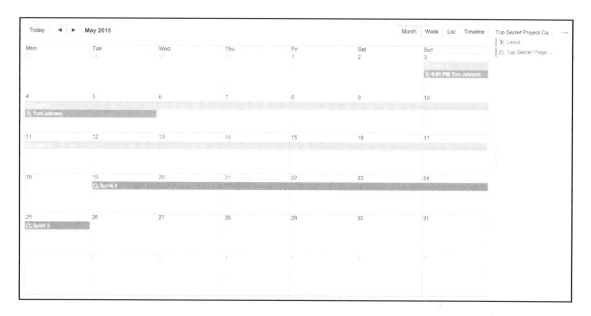

With the calendar all set up, you can also share and embed it. A good way to use this feature is to create a new Confluence page in the same project space where you have all your requirements documentation, call it something like **Project Calendar**, and then embed the calendar into the page. To embed the calendar into a page:

1. Click on the **Create** button at the top of the page.
2. Select the project space for the **Select space** field.
3. Now select the **Blank page** option and click on the **Create** button.
4. Name the page **Project Calendar**.
5. Select and add the **Team Calendar** macro into the page.
6. Click on the **Add Existing Calendar** option.
7. Search for the calendar you have created, and click on the **Add** button.

8. Click on the **Save** button to create the page:

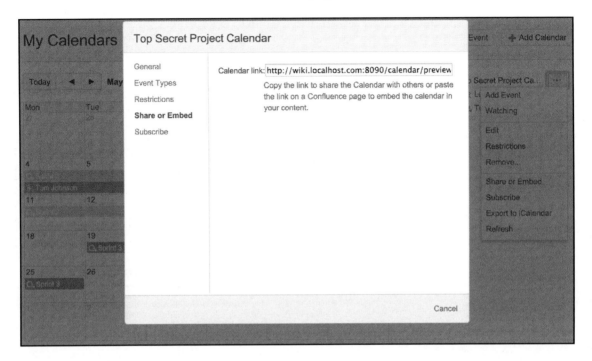

After you have created the page, you will have all the information about the project in a single place along with the Confluence space for the project, for easy access. One additional step you can take is to create a quick shortcut link on your Scrum board to the **Project Calendar** page, so it is just a click away when you need it.

To create a link to the page:

1. Browse to your Scrum board.
2. Click on the **Add link** option from the left-hand side.
3. Enter the URL for the **Project Calendar** page.
4. Enter a label for the link; that is, **Project Calendar**.
5. Click on the **Add** button to create the link.

The link will be displayed under the **Project Shortcuts** section on the left-hand side, as shown in the following screenshot. So during your sprint planning sessions, or work sessions on the active sprint, you can easily access **Project Calendar** and get the most up-to-date information:

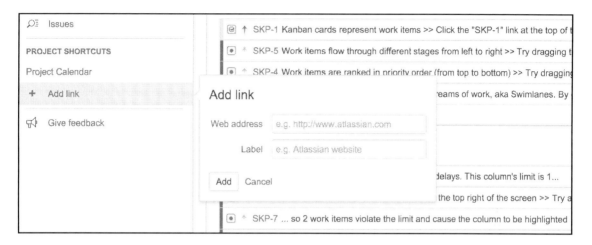

Capturing sprint meeting notes

As we have seen, you can plan and visualize your sprints with Confluence's Team Calendar. Another important part of your sprint planning session is to keep records of the meetings, capturing what was discussed, decisions made, and being able to reference back to those meeting notes in the context of your sprints.

Just like requirement documents, Confluence is also a great place to capture and store this information. From inside your Scrum board, you can create and link each sprint to pages in Confluence, just like with epics. To create a meeting note for a sprint:

1. Browse to your Scrum board.
2. Click on **Backlog** on the left-hand side to display all your sprints.
3. Click on the **Linked pages** link for the sprint that you want to create a meeting note for.

4. Click on the **Create page** button if you want to create a new meeting note page, or the **Link page** button if you already have the meeting note ready:

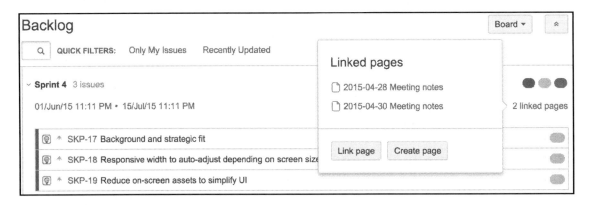

If you click on the **Create page** button, you will be taken to Confluence, with the **Create** dialog showing. It will have the **Meeting notes** blueprint preselected. Make sure the correct space is selected and click on the **Create** button; you will be able to start entering your meeting information. Once you have created and saved the meeting note, the page will have a Jira link referencing the sprint it has been created for, as shown in the following screenshot, and the sprint will also list all the meeting notes it has:

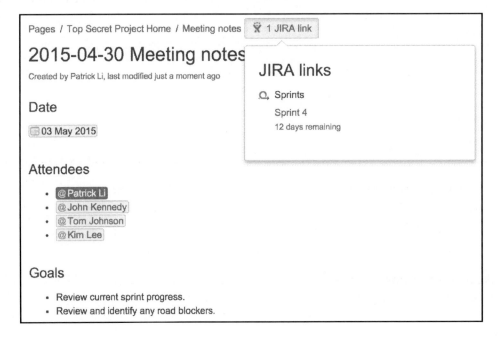

Creating retrospective reports

Other than creating meeting notes, another great feature is being able to create retrospective sprint reports at the end of each sprint. Remember, one of the key ideas behind agile is continuous improvement, so it is important that at the end of each sprint, the entire team comes together and discusses what the they did well, and what went wrong during the sprint; and also to summarize lessons learned and discuss how to improve the process in the next sprint as a team.

To create a retrospective report for your sprint, perform the following steps:

1. Browse to your Scrum board.
2. Click on **Reports** from the left-hand side.
3. Select the sprint to be reported on and select **Sprint Report**.
4. Click on the **Linked pages** link.
5. Click on the **Create page** button:

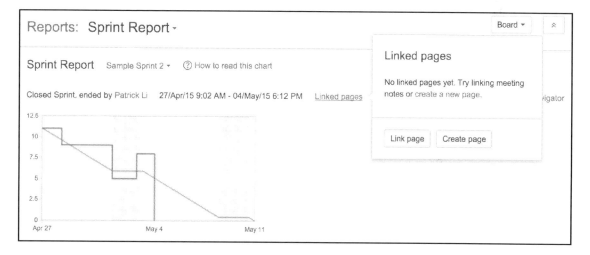

6. Click on the **Next** button in the Confluence **Create** dialog.
7. Enter a title for the report or leave the default.
8. Add all the team members present in the retrospective meeting.
9. Click on the **Create** button to start work on the report.

Just like all other reports created, a reference link will be created between the report and the sprint, so you can easily go back and forth between the two.

Displaying your project in Confluence

The last integration feature between Jira and Confluence is to create reports on the project based on specific versions. There are two types of reports you can create:

- **Change log report**: The change log report lists out all the issues that are part of a selected version. This saves you the hassle of manually compiling a list of issues and entering them. This is a great way to communicate changes within a given version to your customers and other stakeholders.
- **Status report**: The status report is a live report that shows the status of the project in a number of pie charts.

To create these reports, you will start in Confluence instead of Jira:

1. Log into Confluence and browse to your project space.
2. Click on the **Create** button at the top or press the C key on your keyboard.
3. Select **Jira Report** from the **Create** dialog and click on **Create**.
4. Choose the report you want to create and click the **Next** button. In our example, we are creating a status report:

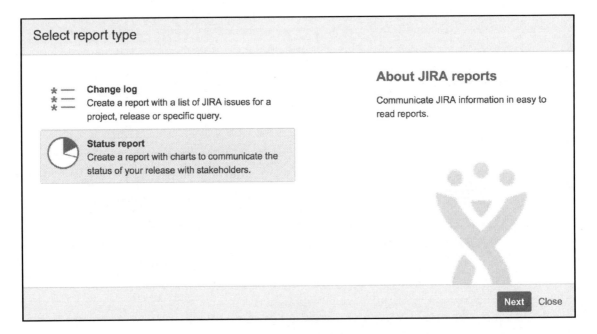

5. Select the project and version to report on. These fields are autopopulated based on data coming from Jira.
6. Enter a title for the report.
7. Click on the **Create** button to start work on the report.

The default report template will be autopopulated based on the information you have provided, so you can simply click on the **Save** button to create the report without any further changes. The following screenshot shows a default status report:

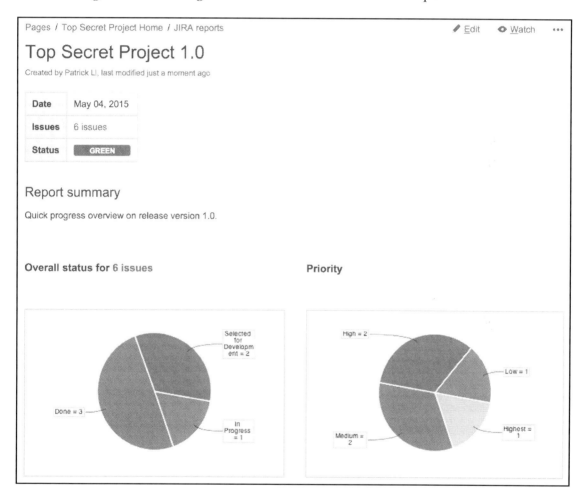

Working with Jira agile boards offline

Jira brings the power of agile to a web-based system where progress and reports can be accessed and shared with everyone, even if they aren't physically colocated together. However, sometimes it is still useful to have a physical board and cards so meetings such as daily stand-ups can feel more interactive and refreshing, rather than having everyone stare at a computer monitor all the time.

This can be done with a third-party add-on called **Agile Cards** - printing issues from Jira. You can search and install it from the **Universal Plugin Manager** (UPM), or download it from the following link, and upload it to Jira via the UPM manually:

`https://marketplace.atlassian.com/plugins/com.spartez.scrumprint.scrumplugin`

Once you have installed the **Agile Cards** add-on, you will see a new print icon added to your boards. The following screenshot shows the new icon in the **Backlog** view of a Scrum board. The icon is also available in the **Active** sprints mode and on the Kanban board:

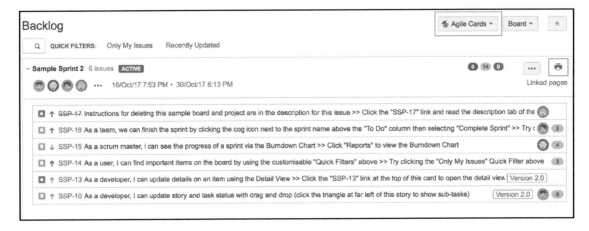

The `print` function is also available outside of Jira; for example, when you run a search in Issue Navigator, or when viewing individual issues.

When you click on the print icon, a new tab will be opened, and each issue will be turned into a card, as shown in the following screenshot:

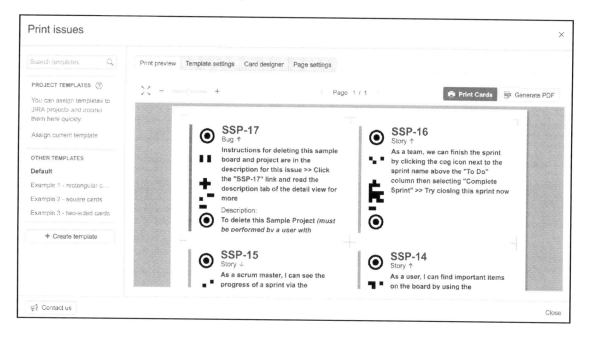

After you have printed your Agile Cards, you can cut them up and pin them onto your physical board, and use them in your team meetings. The second feature of this add-on is that it also allows you to synchronize your physical board with your agile board, by letting you take a photo of your board, and then import that back into Jira.

In order to transfer contents from your physical board to Jira's agile board, we need to add a new piece of information to your physical board, called a **splitter**. A splitter is a piece of paper you need to place between each column on your physical board, so when you take a photo of your physical board, Agile Cards will be able to work out how the columns match up with Jira's agile board. To generate splitters for your board:

1. Browse to the agile board you want to synchronize with.
2. Select the new **Agile Cards** menu and then the **Synchronize physical task board** option.

3. Click the **Physical board setup** tab if this is the first time you are synchronizing both boards:

4. Drag all the columns from the left-hand side that have a corresponding column on your physical board to the **Physical board layout** section.
5. Click the **Print splitters** button to print out splitters.

6. Pin the splitter images onto your physical board, as shown in the following image. This will help Agile Cards to determine which column each card belongs to:

With your physical board all set up with splitters, you can now synchronize with your Jira agile board:

1. Take a photo off your board, and send it to your computer.
2. Go to the agile board you want to synchronize with.
3. Select the new **Agile Cards** menu and then the **Synchronize physical task board** option.
4. Click the **Board synchronization** tab.

5. Select and upload the photo taken from Step 1. If the photo is processed successfully, you will get a summary of all the changes.

6. Review the result and click on the **automatically change status** link to update all issues, or the **bulk edit** links for each column and process them individually.

Agile Cards has several other customization options, such as letting you customize the layout of your card so you can decide what fields will be included in the printout. You can find out more at https://confluence.spartez.com/x/GwAt.

Summary

In this chapter, we looked at some of the additional features and capabilities Jira offers, so you can now create your Scrum and Kanban boards just the way you want them. We looked at using some of the non-agile specific features of Jira, such as gadgets and dashboards to better surface data and help with collaboration. We looked at integrating Jira with Confluence and Team Calendars, so you can create detailed documentations and report and cross-reference them with epics, user stories, and sprints.

Remember, a bit part of these features is to take the data out of Jira so it is not in a silo, and share the information with the team and other stakeholders of your projects. By sharing information on a dashboard, and retrospectively reviewing your progress as a team, you can contiguously refine and improve together, and become successful at using agile and being agile.

In the next chapter, we will look at integrating Jira with Atlassian Bitbucket, another solution from Atlassian that focuses on helping software engineers manage, build, and deploy code. Together with Jira, this will complete the cycle of using Jira Software as an agile project management solution for software development.

7
Jira Software – Release and Deploy

In the previous chapters, we looked at integrating Jira with some other tools from both Atlassian and third-party developers to extend what Jira can do. In this chapter, we will look into using another Atlassian tool called Bamboo to tie together the release, build, and deploy process for a software development project.

By the end of the chapter, you will have learned how to:

- Integrate Jira and Bamboo
- Perform version release and build directly in Jira
- Display build information inside Jira
- Deploy released builds to your operational environments

Integrating Jira with Bamboo

Bamboo is the continuous integration and build server from Atlassian. By integrating Jira and Bamboo together, you can make Jira's issue information available in Bamboo, as well as Bamboo's build and deploy information in Jira.

Setting up an application link with Bamboo

Similar to integrating Jira with Confluence, you need to create a new application link between Jira and Bamboo. To create an application link with Bamboo, perform the following steps:

1. Browse to the Jira administration console.
2. Select the **Applications** tab and then the **Application links** option.
3. Enter the URL to your Bamboo instance and click on the **Create new link** button, as shown in the next screenshot:

4. Tick the **The servers have the same set of users and usernames** option if both Jira and Bamboo share the same user repository; for example, LDAP.
5. Tick the **I am an administrator on both instances** option if you have an administrator account on both Jira and Bamboo. This will let you also create a reciprocal link from Bamboo to Jira.

6. Click on the **Continue** button:

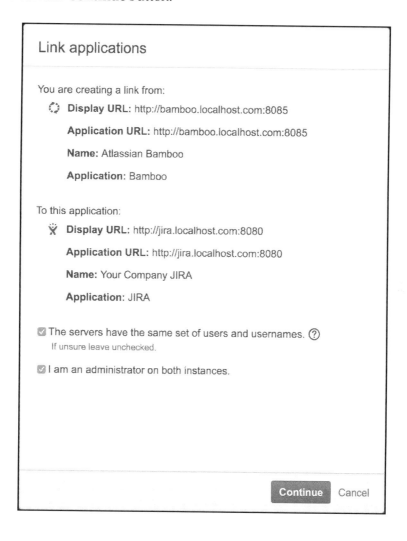

7. Verify that the onscreen information is correct. If both applications are able to communicate with each other successfully, it will display the URLs and application name and type, as shown in the following screenshot. Then, click on the **Continue** button:

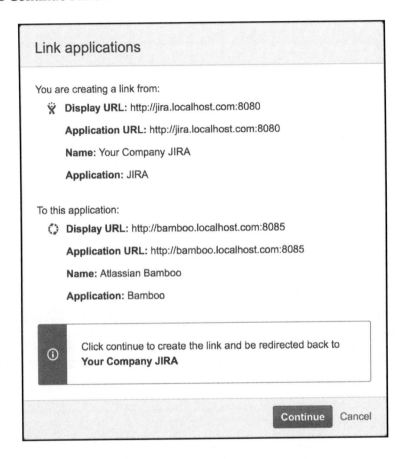

8. Continue with the onscreen wizard, and once the application link is successfully created, you will see a success message and the new application link listed for Bamboo:

Releasing a build from Jira

With Jira and Bamboo integrated, we will be able to combine the process of release in Jira, and build in Bamboo together:

1. Browse to the Jira project you want to run a release for.
2. Click the **Releases** option from the left panel. The **Releases** page should list all the unreleased versions by default, as follows:

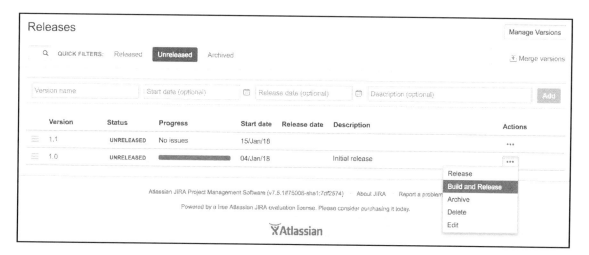

3. Click the **Build and Release** option for the version to release.
4. Select the **with new build** option on the **Release** dialog.
5. Select the build plan to use for building this release. The build plans should be pulled from Bamboo. If you do not see the build plan you want, make sure you have access to the build plan in Bamboo and the application link between Jira and Bamboo are working properly.
6. Click the **Release** button to release and build the version. You do not need to enter a release date, as Jira will automatically fill in today's date for you once the release ID is completed:

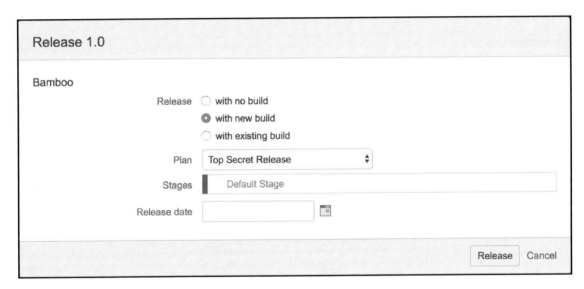

Once the build is completed on Bamboo's side, Jira will mark the version as released, and show you the success result from the build, as follows. You can click on the build result link from this page to go directly to Bamboo and view more detailed information about the build, and perform a release deployment, as we will see later in this chapter:

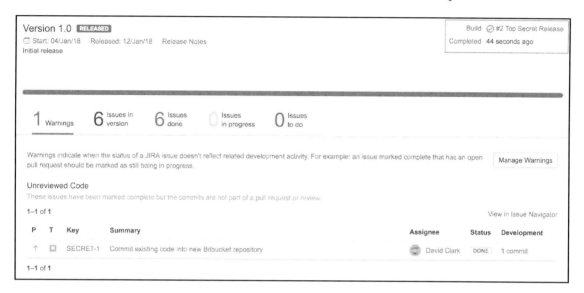

Also, any issues that are related in this release build will also have the build results displayed under the **Development** section, as follows. You can click on that to view the result of the build directly in Jira:

Deploying the release

Once you have successfully built your project, you can also deploy the final built artifact to your environments. There are several ways you can do this. For example, you can have a custom deployment stage as part of your build plan. However, we will be using the deployment plan feature in Bamboo. This gives you more control about how you want to run your deployment process, as well as keeping track of all the deployments you run, and lets you rollback to a previous deployed version if there is a problem.

Setting up a deployment plan

The first step is to set up a new deployment plan in Bamboo:

1. Log into Bamboo.
2. Select the **Create deployment project** option from the **Create** menu.
3. Enter a name for the new deployment project, and select the **Build plan** and branch used to build your project with:

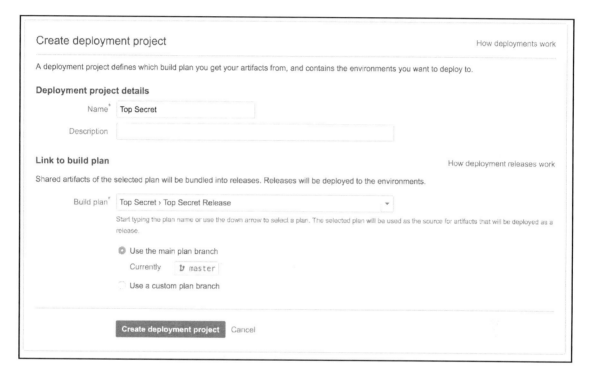

4. Click the **Create deployment project** button to create the deployment plan.
5. With the deployment project created, you will be asked to create an environment. You should create one for each real operational environment you have, such as one for production, and one for testing.

6. Click on the **Continue to task setup** button:

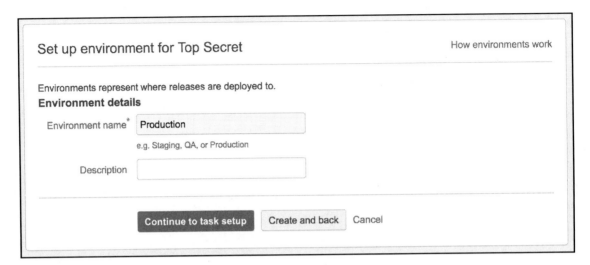

 You will only see artifacts listed if you have defined a shared artifact in your build plan.

7. For each environment, you need to configure the series of tasks to run as part of your deployment. For example, if you are deploying a Java-based web application, you will need to use the **Artifact download** task, and select the artifact created as part of your build process:

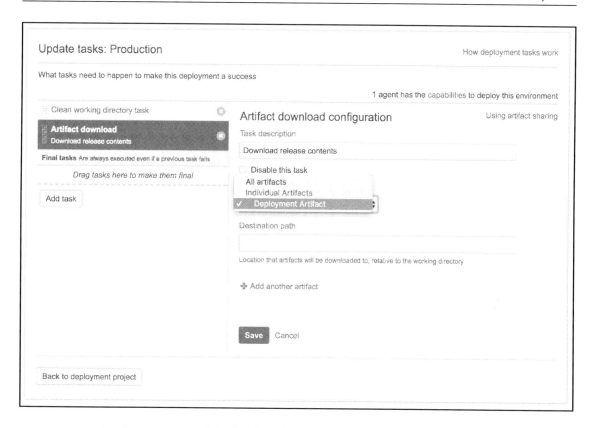

Update tasks: Production

How deployment tasks work

What tasks need to happen to make this deployment a success

1 agent has the capabilities to deploy this environment

Clean working directory task

Artifact download
Download release contents

Final tasks Are always executed even if a previous task fails

Drag tasks here to make them final

Add task

Artifact download configuration

Using artifact sharing

Task description

Download release contents

Disable this task
All artifacts
Individual Artifacts
✓ Deployment Artifact

Destination path

Location that artifacts will be downloaded to, relative to the working directory

⊕ Add another artifact

Save   Cancel

Back to deployment project

Make sure you click the **Save** button for each task before you add a new task.

8. Click on the **Add task** button to add more tasks to your build plan. Bamboo comes with a number of deployment tasks you can use out of the box, such as deploying to Heroku cloud, and using Docker. If you do not see a deployment task suitable for your type of deployment needs, you can also check Atlassian Marketplace, where you will find many more add-ons for Bamboo that have support for other deployment options:

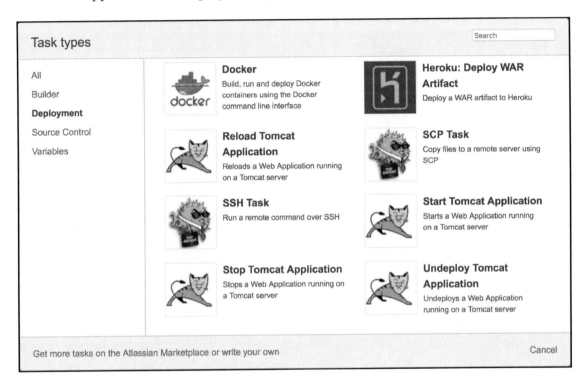

Running the deployment

After we have the deployment plan and target environments created, we can proceed to deploy the released project:

1. Browse to the build result for the release in Bamboo. You can go there from Jira's release page.

2. Click the **Create release** button:

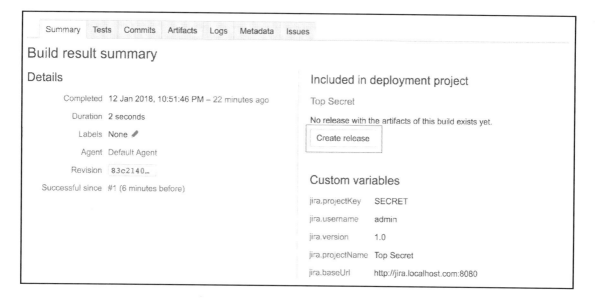

3. Make sure the correct build result is selected.

4. Enter the release version number for this release. This way, we create a history of all the deployments, so we can keep track of the released and deployed version for each environment, and easily rollback in the future. In the following example, we are releasing version 1.0.

5. Click the **Create release** button:

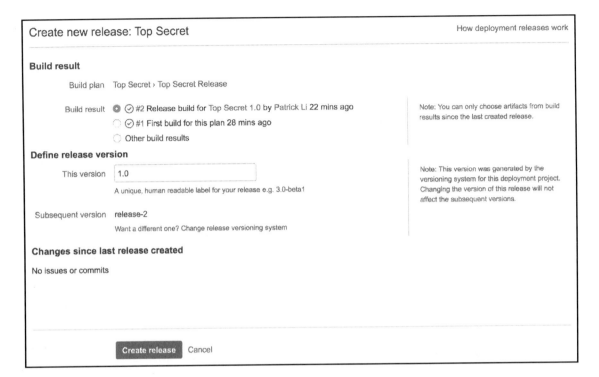

If you have more than one environment, such as testing and production, you should always start with the testing environment first. If the deployment is successful, you will be able to then promote the deployment to production.

6. Select the environment you want to deploy to from the **Deploy** menu. Every environment created earlier should be listed here:

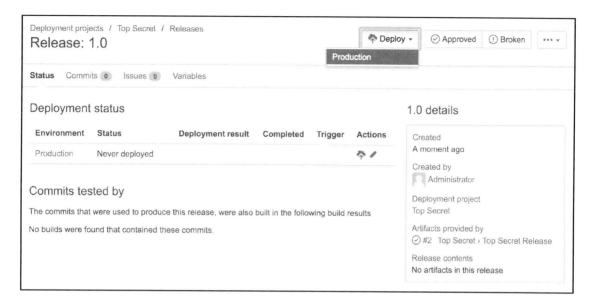

7. Review the deployment and click on the **Start deployment** button to start. Depending on the type of deployment, this can take several minutes or longer to complete. Bamboo will display the deployment progress during all this:

8. If the deployment is successful, you will see the success page as follows. You can promote the deployment to other environments if you need to.

9. Click the **Approved** button if all your post-deployment verification passes. This will mark the deployment as a success:

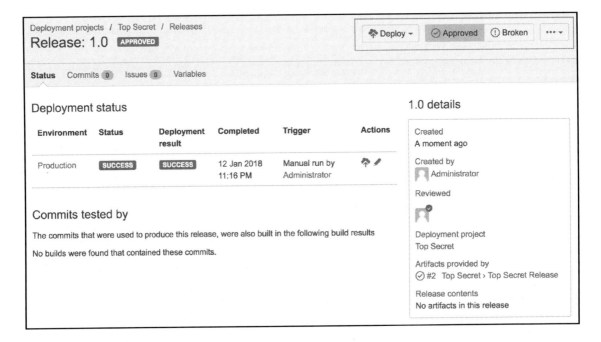

Summary

In this chapter, we looked at Bamboo and what it can do. We used an application link to integrate Jira with Bamboo, so both applications can share information with each other; for example, letting you run build plans from inside Jira. We also looked into Bamboo when setting up a deployment plan, so you can deploy project artifacts you have released and built.

There are many more things you will find you can do with Jira and Bamboo integrated together; for example, you will start seeing build results flowing through automatically into Jira's activity stream on the dashboard, so everyone can be made aware if a build fails. Your build engineers can also view Jira's issue information from inside Bamboo builds, so they can easily pinpoint the cause of build plan failures.

Index

Printed in Great Britain
by Amazon